nnual 2001

Table of Contents

Stop, Look and Listen: How Not to Get Burned on What You Buy / *By Sharon Korbeck* 5
Good, Bad or Mint: Grading a Toy's Condition 5
Flyin' Off the Shelves: The Hottest Toys of 2000 / *By Tom Bartsch* 6
Champagne Dreams: Toy Anniversaries / *By Tom Bartsch* 9
The Class of 2000: "Toy Shop's" Top Picks of the Year 12
Millennium Hits Toy Giants Hard: State of the Industry Report / *By Sharon Korbeck* 14
Market Update: A Look at the 2000 Secondary Toy Market / *By Angelo Van Bogart* 16
Top 10 Boomer Toys: Did Your Favorites Make Our List? / *By Angelo Van Bogart* 22
Make War, Make Money: Military Toys Prevail in 2000 26
Auction Action 2000 / *By Angelo Van Bogart and Tom Bartsch* 28
Wave of the Future: Internet Provides Toys and Prices with a Single Click / *By Tom Bartsch* 38
Toy Dealer Directory 45
Web Site Directory 49
Manufacturers Directory 54
2001 Toy Show Calendar 61

Foreword

Last year at this time, many people were planning parties to celebrate the new year (and the arguable turn of the century, which by most accounts doesn't *really* begin until 2001). Bashes were big; Y2K concerns were, mostly, unfounded; and the world kept turning.

Now as we greet the real new millennium, we in the toy industry have chosen to both look back and forge forward. More than ever, toys of the past year have embraced technology — do we honestly need *another* robotic dog?

But 2000 was also a year to look back at the evergreen toys that have enthused generations . . . and continue to do so. Mark Rich's recent book, *100 Greatest Baby Boomer Toys*, set us on the path to remembering toys like Slinky, Mr. Potato Head, Barbie, Hot Wheels, Marx play sets and more. Want to know if your favorites made Rich's top 10 list? Check out our story on page 22.

In this annual, we also look back on some of our favorite older toys, like the classic cast-iron, Disney wind-ups and antique dolls that commanded top prices at auctions.

In addition to features looking back on the year in toys, you'll also find helpful directories of toy manufacturers and dealers. A complete 2001 show calendar and a guide to toy Web sites are also included.

Enjoy our look back at toy collecting in the last year of the century.

Sharon Korbeck
korbecks@krause.com

Toy Shop Annual 2001

Editor: Sharon Korbeck (korbecks@krause.com)
Associate Editor: Tom Bartsch (bartscht@krause.com)
Cover design by Tom Dupuis

Visit us online at www.krause.com or www.toyshopmag.com

Copyright © 2001 by Krause Publications
ISBN 0-87341-998-7. Published in the United States of America by Krause Publications, 700 E. State St., Iola, WI 54990-0001, 715-445-2214, www.krause.com, publishers of *Toy Shop* magazine. Krause Publications cannot accept liability for typographical errors. The entire contents of the *Toy Shop Annual 2001* are copyright © Krause Publications and may not be reproduced in any form without express written consent from the publisher. All rights reserved.

Advertiser Index

Mark Bergin	.41
Best Comics	.25
CRM2000	.41
Hamilton-Wilber	.41
Joe Depot	.41
Krause Publications	.40, 42
Krause Publications	.43, 44
Krause Publications	.73, 74
Sonos Models	.40

Stop, Look and Listen
How Not to Get Burned on Your Buy

By Sharon Korbeck

The long-held tenet of fire safety is "stop, drop and roll."

However, if you don't want to get burned on your next toy purchase, consider this rule — "stop, look and listen."

1. Stop. Walking down the third aisle of a mile-long collectibles show, you've just spotted it — that long-anticipated, impossibly hard-to-find toy. Maybe it's that Hopalong Cassidy holster set you need to complete your collection. Maybe it's a Batgirl Super Queens figure. Maybe it's a Volkswagen Beach Bomb with — gasp! — surfboards in the back.

Once you check your obvious excitement and calm down enough to bargain, stop a moment to consider a few things.

Is the asking price reasonable? If it is, is it a price you're willing to pay to add that coveted item to your collection?

We've all been in this situation. Even if $200 is a fair asking price for the toy of your dreams, do you have (or want to spend) the money?

2. Look. Look closely at the toy to determine its true condition. Is it in a condition you can live with . . . or do you only want to acquire Mint items? Is the toy ultimately too rare and desirable to pass up? Will you kick yourself after leaving if you don't buy it?

Looking closely isn't always possible when buying from an ad in print or online. Pictures don't always accurately represent the true condition of the toy. As carefully as possible, examine the pictures of the toy, and ask questions as necessary.

3. Listen. Any questions concerning price, condition, authenticity or provenance should be sufficiently answered by the seller. Listen closely to what the seller says. Does he/she really know the item is authentic? Can he/she prove it? Where was it originally purchased? Was it restored or repaired?

Granted, a seller may not know the answers to some of these questions, but they are fair game for buyers to ask.

The decision whether or not to buy is ultimately yours — but taking the time to stop, look and listen could save you time, money and headaches.

Good, Bad or Mint? Grading a Toy's Condition

All toys are not created equal. And because of this, there are different factors to consider before buying an action figure, die-cast car, Barbie doll or vintage tin wind-up. Here are the basics to look for.

1. Packaging. Most toys packaged on original cards or in original boxes command higher prices than those outside the box. Questions to ask yourself about packaging include — Does the box exhibit shelf wear? Are the edges worn or lightened in color? Does a blister card have a crease or scratches? Is the plastic bubble perfect?

2. Material. What is the toy made of and how sturdy is that material? For example, paper items (like boxes, paper dolls and coloring books) will likely exhibit some wear over time. Some wear on these items may be acceptable to collectors; major wear, however, may not. Cast-iron toys, which should have held up better over time, should be judged differently than toys made of less-sturdy construction.

3. Age of Item. When was the toy originally made? Late 1800s? 1950s? 1990s? A collector buying a toy from the early 1900s may be willing to accept a lesser-condition item since so few examples may still exist (and the toy has had to survive over 90 years). But toys from the past 20 years often must be in much better condition to entice buyers, unless the toy is ultra-rare or desirable.

4. Appearance and Function. These two factors are often vital to the collector, and they go hand in hand. For example, a vintage Fisher-Price pull toy may look great, but does it work as it was originally intended? Some collectors may not care whether or not a toy is operational as long as it looks good for display purposes.

Dealers and publications use various grading systems, but the basic tenets of condition and appearance apply, although perhaps at different levels. For example, the O'Brien's *Collecting Toys* books use a C6, C8, C10 grading system, which compares fairly closely to well-established Good, Excellent and Mint conditions.

Decide what type of collector you want to be — the level of money you are willing to spend, the amount of return (if any) you hope to reap from your investments and the amount of time you will devote to your hobby.

So, learn the jargon, develop a sharp eye for subtleties, compare grading scales and decide what a toy is worth to you. You can turn the subjective field of toy collecting into a rewarding objective for yourself.

Flyin' Off the Shelves
Movies, TV Spark the Top Toys of the Year

By Tom Bartsch

Robotic dogs that obey your every command. Poseable female action figures fighting for justice. A chance for fans to control the actions of their favorite boy band.

These, along with interactive pets and new twists to familiar toy favorites, helped make this an interesting and active year for the toy market.

Movies were a big influence this year, with such blockbusters as *X-Men*; *Charlie's Angels*; *Chicken Run*; *Austin Powers, The Spy Who Shagged Me* and the television shows *Survivor* and *Who Wants to be a Millionaire?* providing the backdrop for many popular toys.

Toy Shop's picks of the top 10 toys of the year, like Playmates' Simpsons figure and the X-Men line from Toy Biz, can be found on page 12. Here's a look at some of the other toys that have created extra traffic at retail outlets.

Austin Powers — One of the more popular lines this year included the *Austin Powers* line from McFarlane Toys. With a pull-string talking mechanism, characters like Fat Bastard and Dr. Evil speak lines from the movie. Their incredible likeness to the on-screen characters is yet another draw for collectors and fans alike.

Chicken Run — The clay-animated wonder from Aardman Animations featuring the fleeing fowl was a treat for viewers and for the toy market. Playmates unveiled its line of action figures, including Rocky, Ginger and the rest of the characters, who try to escape the chicken death trap known as the Tweedy Chicken Farm.

Playmates offered collectible three-packs, gift sets and assortments of the figures.

WWF Figures — Not a night goes by when they're not seen on television. From their wrestling matches to guest appearances at presidential party nomination ceremonies, WWF wrestlers are as popular as ever.

To capitalize on their success, JAKKS Pacific issued its Series 5 figures, with real scan technology to provide even greater likenesses to the wrestlers in the ring.

Until the ratings start to sour, these figures could be an annual lock on everyone's best of the year lists.

Matilda — Yes, the name sounds matronly, but that stereotype couldn't be further from the truth.

Playing Mantis brought two genres of collectors together with its Monopoly cars.

Matilda reigns supreme among this year's female action figures.

Chicken Run figures from Playmates brought the clay-animated characters to life.

Halloween may be just once a year, but fans of the movie can celebrate all year long with this Polar Lights model kit.

Matilda is part of The Villains line from 21st Century Toys and packs an assortment of weapons to fend off her opponents.

Matilda is one of the more requested action figures today, a sign that female action figures are starting to rival their male counterparts in popularity with collectors.

Monopoly cars — The die-cast hobby is hotter than ever. Combine that with one of the most popular board games of all time, and you have an instant hit. Johnny Lightning teamed up with Hasbro to produce a dozen 1:64 scale Monopoly cars.

All your favorites are presented from the Reading Railroad Ford Truck to the Do Not Pass Go Crown Victoria. Plus, collectors get new playing pieces for the board game. Each car comes with a matching game token.

Michael Myers model kit — Some movie characters are known for their looks. Others for their memorable roles or mannerisms. And then there are those characters that generate fear simply by uttering the name.

Michael Myers of *Halloween* fame (not the funny man Mike Myers) was offered this year in model kit form by Playing Mantis/Polar Lights. The character that made Haddonfield, Ill., famous had fans clamoring for his 1:10th-scale likeness.

The diorama, complete with a decorated porch base, jack-o'-lantern, spilled candy bag, knife and child's mask, add to the appeal.

Charlie's Angels dolls — Straight from the '70s come those high-kickin' super sleuths known as Charlie's Angels. In a remake of the popular television show, *Charlie's Angels* made its big-screen debut in fall, 2000, but the dolls spurred interest long before that.

Made in the likenesses of the movie's three stars, Lucy Liu (Alex), Cameron Diaz (Natalie) and Drew Barrymore (Dylan), the dolls transform to all the right poses and look good doing it. Think you will get bored with the same outfits on the dolls? Don't worry, accessories are available to have the wardrobes match the crime that needs to be solved.

Poo-Chi — Usually toys are inanimate objects that only obey orders through the imagination. Not any more.

If you don't want a real pet, a mechanical likeness is the next best thing. In a wave of interactive toys, namely pets, comes this Tiger Electronics product.

This pooch has a bag of new tricks to show off as it sings, plays games, stands, sits and dances. With its advanced technology, Poo-Chi also responds to its owner emotion-

 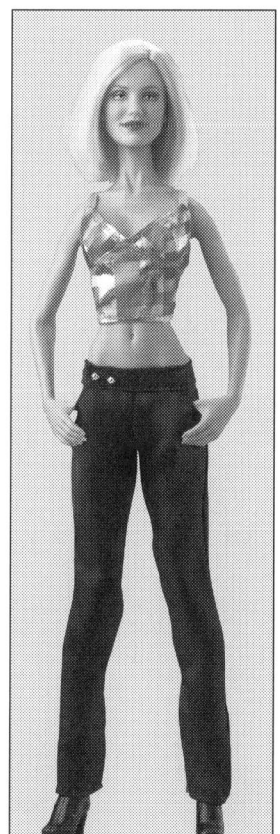 

The high kickin', head turnin' vixens of "Charlie's Angels" are available as dolls compliments of JAKKS Pacific.

ally and senses light, sound and touch.

And if Poo-Chi isn't interactive enough, also available is Super Poo-Chi. No word yet if either is potty-trained.

N'Sync Marionettes — They're hot, young and taking the world by storm. In the latest batch of boy bands, N'Sync has offered its fans a unique collectible — life-like marionettes from Living Toyz. You can pick your favorite band member or collect all five. Either way, you now get to control their every command.

The marionettes were produced in conjunction with N'Sync's popular-selling, and appropriately named, album *No Strings Attached*.

Righty the Elephant — Though the Beanie Baby market is nowhere near where it once stood, some characters continue to draw collectors.

In conjunction with the presidential race this year, Ty Inc. released Righty the Elephant Beanie Buddy. Partnering up with Lefty the Donkey, the duo helped spread the word of the upcoming election and provided Ty collectors with another addition to the ever-growing family of Beanie products.

Tonka's Tucker My Talkin' Truckbot has all the bells and whistles and phrases and sound effects to keep kids happy until next year's top toys debut.

Surprise, surprise. One of the best toys of the year was McFarlane's Fat Bastard from "Austin Powers 2."

Who Wants to be a Millionaire? — It doesn't come with a voice-activated Regis, which might be a good thing, but it comes with the same thought-provoking questions as the hit television show.

Produced by Pressman, the game allows players to go for the million or walk away with just enough to pay for that dream house. Of course the money isn't real but the questions and drama are straight from the show. All the lifelines are available, and there are more than enough questions to keep you guessing for many games to come.

Tucker My Talkin' Truckbot — Not only can Tucker move and haul dirt, which used to make a toy an instant hit, it also speaks, reacts to its owner's actions and encourages play time.

Following the recent trend of interactive toys, Hasbro has produced this colorful and fun toy that takes Tonka trucks to a whole new level. So put on your hard hat and find that dirt mound, Tucker is ready to roll.

Of course, this isn't a complete list of all the great toys introduced in 2000, just some of the top toys out there. To find the rest, just head to your retail outlet and find the treasure chest known as the toy department.

Best Selling Toys of Late 2000

According to the October, 2000, issue of *Playthings*, these were the top 10 best selling toys introduced in the year 2000 (through September).

1. Poo-Chi Robotic Dog, Tiger Electronics
2. Pokémon Rocket Booster, Wizards of the Coast
3. Celebration Barbie, Mattel
4. Who Wants to be a Millionaire? board game, Pressman
5. Pokémon Rocket Deck, Wizards of the Coast
6. Barbie Wizard of Oz Asst., Mattel
7. Wizard of Oz Men Asst., Mattel
8. Mary-Kate and Ashley Asst., Mattel
9. Barbie Secret Messages, Mattel

Champagne Wishes

Lionel, Raggedy Ann Celebrate Anniversaries

Some people hate them, others see it as a right of passage. For toy companies, as each one passes by it's a step in the right direction, providing stability and recognizability in the toy market.

They're anniversaries, and each year brings a new round of celebrations. The year 2000 was no different, as many familiar faces and toys celebrated another year being coveted by fans.

Here are some of the toys that celebrated anniversaries in 2000.

100 YEARS
Lionel

New York inventor Joshua Lionel Cowen opened a small shop in New York City and made trains to be used as displays for his store. Little did he know then that the Lionel trains he produced to attract customers into his store would go on to be one of the most recognizable toys in the world and be a featured toy in and of itself.

Not many companies can say they survived two world wars and a depression, but Lionel is still chugging after a century of toys.

Since its inception, Lionel has survived two world wars and a depression. Always keeping up with the times, Lionel's 2000 products are the most innovative yet, featuring the new Odyssey System which makes trains seem like they are on cruise control.

A quick fact — to produce the Lionel line, more than 100 million separate parts are used.

85 YEARS
Raggedy Ann

The red-haired, triangle-nosed children's favorite burst on the scene in Johnny Gruelle's *Raggedy Ann Stories* three years after it was patented in 1915.

According to Patricia Hall, author of *Johnny Gruelle, Creator of Raggedy Ann and Andy*, the first Raggedy Ann doll was made by the Gruelle family, without the benefit of advertisements to sell the dolls. Later, the Non-Breakable Toy Co. made the first commercially-produced Raggedy Ann dolls.

The first doll, the "Cottage" Raggedy Ann, is worth between $1,400 and $6,500. Among recent items, Raggedy Ann has a birthday doll edition, and she has also been immortalized on a U.S. postage stamp.

80 YEARS
Raggedy Andy

The famous brother to Raggedy Ann, Raggedy Andy was introduced five years after his sister. They have been inseparable ever since. He first made his appearance in Johnny Gruelle's *Raggedy Andy Stories* as the good-natured sidekick.

Though he's hard to find solo, Raggedy Andy is just as popular and can be found in many collectible shops.

Raggedy Ann and Andy have enjoyed 80 years together.

Toy Shop Annual 2001

A half-century later, the bald kid and beloved beagle, along with the rest of the cast, are still popular.

70 YEARS
Blondie

She continues to run the household, now owns her own catering service and gets Dagwood to work on time. Not bad for being 70 years old.

The popular comic strip created by Chic Young has produced many memorable characters through the years, including the Bumstead's children, Cookie and Alexander, Daisy the dog and Dagwood's boss, Mr. Dithers.

Young drew Blondie for 43 years, accumulating more than 15,000 strips in the process. After his death in 1973, his son, Dean, took over the strip, which is still enjoyed by readers today.

50 YEARS
Peanuts

Charlie Brown running to kick the football as Lucy pulls it away at the last minute. Linus snuggling up to his blue blanket while sucking his thumb. Snoopy masquerading as the World War II flying ace Red Baron. These depictions are all too familiar to the legions of Peanuts fans who have followed the round-headed characters for the past half-century.

The familiar cast of characters have leapt from newspapers to the television screen, and the holiday specials are an annual event for many viewers.

Sadly, creator Charles Schulz passed away the same year *Peanuts* celebrates its half-century as one of the most-read comics. And while no new strips are written, millions are still able to see his work in newspapers each day.

Beetle Bailey

Mort Walker's portrayal of Army life as seen through the characters in his famous comic strip has provided comedic relief to readers and many, many bumps and bruises to poor Beetle, compliments of Sarge.

Walker began the strip as a college cutup until King Features Syndicate picked it up. Soon Beetle and the gang were distributed to more than 1,800 newspapers, many of which still carry the strip.

To celebrate the 50th anniversary of Beetle Bailey, a bunch of licensed collectibles are now available from Equity Marketing, UT Models, Dark

Beetle Bailey celebrates 50 years.

Blondie and her husband Dagwood are still featured in daily newspapers.

Horse Comics and Enesco and others.

Quick fact — Walker's Beetle Bailey was the last comic strip personally approved by William Randolph Hearst.

Silly Putty

It's the toy that can be bounced, rolled and molded. It can even pick up newspaper print. And though the boric acid and silicone oil combination doesn't have all the bells and whistles of today's toys, it's remained a favorite for 50 years.

James Wright came up with the substance while coming up with a rubber substitute during World War II. Though it didn't fly with the government, it eventually found its way into toy store catalogs.

The real break for Silly Putty came when it was mentioned in a column in *The New Yorker*, sending sales through the roof. To celebrate its 50th anniversary, Silly Putty has released a special golden edition and launched a Web site, *www.sillyputty.com*.

40 YEARS
The Game of Life

While some parents wouldn't want their kids to be married with children at age 8 in the real life, this play version allowed kids to be adults. Though Life is determined by the spin of a dial, players got to choose which direction they wanted to take, much like the daily decisions of real life.

The modern game debuted in 1960, but according to *100 Greatest Baby Boomer Toys* (Krause Publications, 2000), it could be 100 years older, when Milton Bradley designed a game called The Checkered Game of Life. That version was updated in its centennial year by Milton Bradley to feature the plastic pieces and landscape seen today. There is even a CD-ROM version today.

The Flintstones

The Stone Age, where leaders were chosen based on their might and "cars" were foot-driven, also spawned a batch of the great television characters known as The Flintstones. Loudmouth Fred and the giggly Wilma made their television debut Sept. 30, 1960, becoming the first prime-time television cartoon.

The Flintstones have since made a leap to the big screen, while the cartoon runs in syndication.

30 YEARS
G.I. Joe Adventure Team

Created as an answer to the military G.I. Joes that went by the wayside courtesy of the Vietnam conflict in the late 1960s, Hasbro's Adventure Team Series gained popularity among the Joe faithful.

Yabba dabba doo, the Flintstones are still rolling.

Some of the figures in the series included the Land Adventurer, Sea Adventurer and Man of Action, and all sported new, life-like hair. The series later added talking features and were the first to include the famous kung-fu grip. The series also was the first to show the resculpted black figure, seen in the series' Black Adventurer.

20 YEARS
Rubik's Cube

The prototype was created in 1974 in Budapest, Hungary, and the Rubik's Cube was introduced to the U.S. in 1980.

It seems so simple. Just match the colors on each of the nine squares on all six sides. Yet frustrated bystanders who decided to pick up the cube soon found that putting together the color scheme was no small task.

Many resorted to peeling off the color squares to wow others, or simply to put the matter at rest. Twenty years later, the toy is still enjoyed by many, with few homes lacking one.

Yes, there are Web sites out there to help Internet surfers "solve" the cube, but is that really what the originator had in mind?

Pac-Man

Though he looks like a pie that has already been taste tested by a hungry person, he remains a fixture in video game lore.

Introduced by Midway in 1980 in two versions, an upright arcade machine along with a cocktail table version, Pac-Man has been eating pellets, and with the help of the special pellets, ghosts, ever since.

Many versions of the fabled game have spun off the original, from Ms. Pac-Man to Super Pac-Man to Pac-Man 2, and most video game systems that come out today still offer the game.

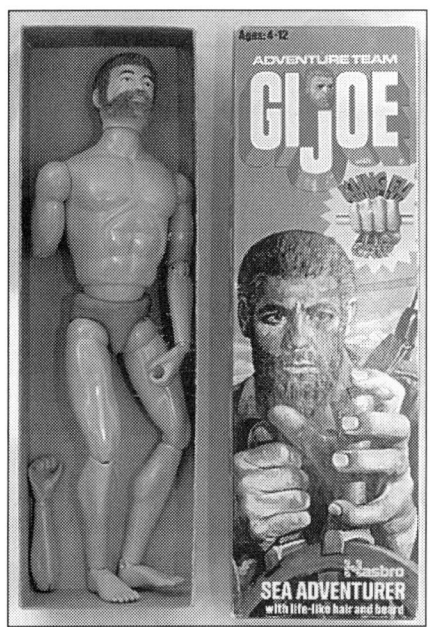

Sea Adventurer was just one member of the G.I. Joe Adventure Team.

Rubik's Cube has provided hours of futility for millions of people. The cube made its initial debut in 1974 in Hungary.

Toy Shop Annual 2001

The Class of 2000
'Toy Shop' Picks its Top Toys for Collectors

The cream of the crop. The kings of the toy box. The pride of a collector's shelf.

The toys listed below are, in *Toy Shop*'s estimation, among the best of the year. We thought long and hard to bring you our picks for 2000. They're toys we feel will remain favorites with collectors far into the future, particularly on the secondary market.

1. Wonder Woman Barbie, Mattel. In her box, this Barbie is a three-dimensional comic book cover. With long flowing black hair, golden lasso and bright blue cape, this doll may be slightly overdressed to fight crime, but she'll look good doing it. This superhero is sure to be spinning off shelves. Invisible jet not included.

2. Where the Wild Things Are, McFarlane Toys. The monsters from Maurice Sendak's classic 1963 children's book, *Where the Wild Things Are*, roar to life under the cunning and clever eye of Todd McFarlane. Every poised arm, every side-glancing eye, every polished horn is exacting, and the subtle packing stays true to the tone of the book. Why didn't someone think of this before?

3. X-Men, Toy Biz. These mutants never had a chance to gather dust on the shelves of stores. After the hit summer movie, the comic book turned Hollywood story was ripe for action figures. Collectors, as well as children, followed with their wallets from the theater to the store to snatch up characters like Jean Grey and Wolverine. Toys R Us exclusives created additional opportunities to catch X-Men fever.

4. John F. Kennedy G.I. Joe, Hasbro. A man already immortalized in American history has been immortalized as an action figure for all to remember. Dressed in a World War II uniform, JFK depicts the role of PT-109 patrol boat commander. The aura around the Kennedy family is sure to make Hasbro's only licensed G.I. Joe this year a winner.

5. Classic Muscle 1:64 die-cast cars, Ertl. Dual exhaust systems that look so real you can almost hear the rumble spitting out the tip. Dashboards and gauges that look as though the radio can crank out your favorite tunes from yesterday. These miniature cars set the standard for accuracy and detail in their respective category.

By bringing back examples from the '50s and '60s, Ertl was able to warm the hearts of muscle car enthusiasts the same way they had with their 1:18 scale series that has

X-Men figures from Toy Biz proved to be as big a hit as the movie.

Superhero meets the famous fashion doll as Mattel's Wonder Woman Barbie.

Some of the most anticipated toys of 2000 come from the Caldecott Award-winning children's book "Where the Wild Things Are" by Maurice Sendak.

already proven popular. Anybody who could bring collectors the mighty Chrysler 300C in 1:64 scale shall earn the praises of many.

6. The Simpsons, Playmates. Any accurate version of a Simpsons toy is a sure thing, and these action figures feature America's favorite dysfunctional cartoon with the appropriate bright colors and poseable appendages. The characters are even placed into their appropriate settings through different dioramas, depending on the character. Marge is at home, complete with the family couch. Homer is available with his desk from the nuclear plant he works at and is complete with his safety helmet. Don't get nuked by missing out on these faithful recreations.

7. Elizabeth Taylor in *Father of the Bride*, Mattel. The ever-popular Liz Taylor became immortalized by Mattel once again this year when they honored her in her role of in the 1950 film *Father of the Bride*. With her elaborate white wedding dress and long, flowing veil, this figure could have come straight off the silver screen. Mattel's doll faithfully recreates Taylor's trademark violet eyes and facial features, making the doll eerily accurate.

8. Harley-Davidson Barbie No. 4, Mattel. This ain't no doll; she's a wind in the face on a lonely desert highway kind of girl. She loves nothing more than strapping on her helmet and straddling the two-wheeled freedom that will rumble her to her next destination.

Mattel's fourth version of the popular Harley Barbie is sure to appeal to not only the Barbie collectors but the Harley crowd as well as it has in the past. Her ever-present boyfriend, Ken, makes his second Harley-Davidson incarnation with a grizzly 5 o'clock shadow, leather chaps and helmet.

Mattel also made a V-Twin powered Fat Boy for these two to ride off into the sunset.

9. American Graffiti 1:18 cars, Ertl. Ron Howard and George Lucas may be big Hollywood names, but to car fans, they were costars in one of the greatest car films of all time. The real stars were Ron Howard's white 1958 Impala sport coupe and the hot rod yellow 1932 Ford five-window coupe driven by Paul Le Mat.

But who can forget Harrison Ford's jet black 1955 Chevrolet 150 coupe as it pursues the deuce, aching for a race? Obviously not Ertl, which has faithfully recreated the details on each car, including the rolled and pleated interior on the Impala and the chopped roof of the Pharaoh's Merc.

10. Universal Monsters, Sideshow Toy. Frankenstein never looked so good. With Sideshow's obvious love and knowledge of monsters, the 12-inch boxed version of this monster came out right. Even the boxes for these figures are works of art, featuring original movie poster art to add to their collectibility.

Honorable Mention: Harry Potter toys. While we hadn't seen many before press time, strong licensees Hasbro, LEGO and Mattel, among others, will be cashing in on the magical powers of this novel hero. After burning up the *New York Times* bestsellers list and a motion picture in the works, this license is the hottest of them all. The earliest toys to look for include Mattel's trivia game, cold-cast figures and Warner Bros. Studio Store's costume.

"Toy Shop" magazine editorial staff Sharon Korbeck, Tom Bartsch, Elizabeth Stephan, Merry Dudley and Angelo Van Bogart contributed to this story.

America's favorite family can now join yours with Playmates' popular "Simpsons" figures.

Harley-Davidson Barbie No. 4.

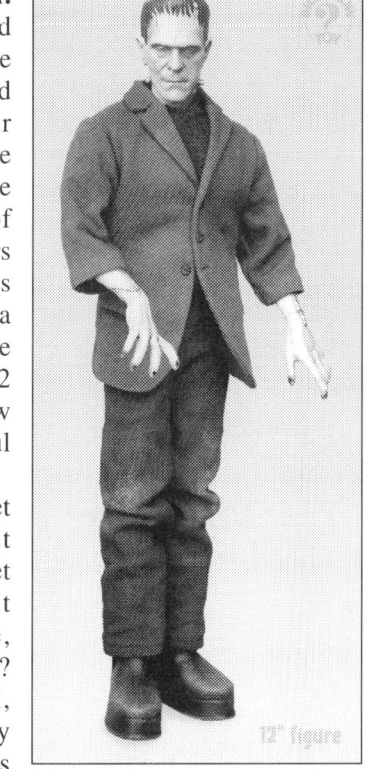
Sideshow Toy's 12-inch Frankenstein.

Millennium Hits Toy Giants Hard
Layoffs Plague Hasbro; Mattel Loses CEO

By Sharon Korbeck

The start of the new millennium opened with consequence for the world's top two toymakers.

And while technology continues to change the face of the toy industry, it was that same technology which ushered in peril for both Hasbro and Mattel.

As the year 2000 dawned, Hasbro announced it would eliminate 2,200 jobs (19 percent of its workforce), citing the need to offer more interactive toys.

The world's second-largest toymaker planned on closing plants in Tijuana, Mexico, and Ashford, England.

Much of the company's manufacturing takes place in Asia, where a large number of technology-related items are produced. Of the 2,200 jobs, about 1,850 were manufacturing positions.

Like many toy companies, Hasbro had increased efforts in recent years to produce toys that are interesting and challenging for today's computer-literate children.

Hasbro officials said the reorganization will enable them to better focus on expanding its interactive offerings and brands, which include Wizards of the Coast trading cards (including Pokémon); Tiger Electronics, which produces Furby; and Tonka trucks.

Hasbro officials said the restructuring will generate savings of $16 million in 2000 and $23 million a year after that.

Interestingly, a mere 10 months later, the weak performance of Hasbro's interactive toys sector prompted another layoff.

In October, the company announced it would close three of its U.S. offices, cutting 500 to 550 jobs.

The anticipated cut was approximately 5 percent of the company's global workforce.

The No. 2 U.S. toymaker hoped the move would "reduce fixed overhead, enhance our speed to market and improve the product development process, helping us grow our core brands," said Alfred J. Verrecchia, Hasbro's president and COO.

"Our first step is to close our toy facilities in Cincinnati, Ohio, and in Napa and San Francisco, Calif., and to consolidate the U.S. toy group into Rhode Island," Verrecchia said. Hasbro's headquarters is in Pawtucket, R.I.

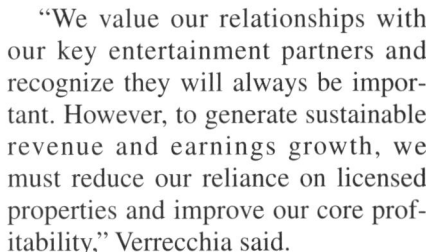

According to Hasbro Chairman and CEO Alan G. Hassenfeld, "Improving Hasbro's profitability is our highest priority. I am confident we are making the right moves to help make Hasbro leaner and more consistently profitable for our shareholders."

Hasbro had anticipated second half results would be below expectations, reflecting soft demand for Pokémon toys in the U.S. and Star Wars worldwide, continuing weakness in the Hasbro Interactive area and other factors.

Weak sales of the licensed products mentioned led Hasbro to focus its attention on core brands and "mitigate some of the risk factors" involved in teaming with licensors.

"We value our relationships with our key entertainment partners and recognize they will always be important. However, to generate sustainable revenue and earnings growth, we must reduce our reliance on licensed properties and improve our core profitability," Verrecchia said.

This may affect Hasbro's future licenses, and some anticipated licenses could be cancelled, according to Verrecchia.

Upcoming 2001 licenses Hasbro has secured include Disney's *Monster's Inc.*, *Jurassic Park 3* and *Harry Potter and the Sorcerer's Stone*.

Major brand names under the Hasbro umbrella include Kenner (a now-defunct brand name), Playskool, Tonka, Tiger, Galoob, Milton Bradley, Parker Brothers, Hasbro Interactive and Wizards of the Coast.

Hasbro Signs with Disney

Late 2000 news saw The Walt Disney Co. and Hasbro reach a multi-year agreement which allowed Hasbro to become the official toy and game company for Walt Disney World Resort, Disneyland Resort and Disneyland Paris Resort.

The agreement also called for Hasbro to develop and market toys and games for upcoming Disney-branded films, starting with *Monsters Inc.*, scheduled for a fall 2001 release.

The agreement allowed Hasbro to produce plush toys, action figures, vehicles, games, dolls and more. Hasbro's products and name will also be showcased at Disney's theme parks and resorts.

Mattel's CEO Leaves

Hasbro wasn't the only company feeling the impact of weakening sales of technology/interactive toys.

In early 2000, Mattel's CEO of three years, Jill Barad, stepped down in the wake of dismal earnings and an anticipated poor fourth quarter.

Published reports said Mattel had struggled since the 1999 purchase of The Learning Co., a software company.

Barad was replaced by Robert Eckert later in 2000.

McFarlane Sued, Loses... then Wins

In mid-2000, *Spawn* creator Todd McFarlane was embroiled in a lawsuit filed by former St. Louis Blues hockey player Tony Twist. McFarlane lost the suit and was ordered to pay $24.5 million.

On Halloween, Judge Robert H. Dierker threw out the judgment, stating the case lacked "credible evidence that McFarlane at any time intended to injure Twist's marketability, to capitalize on the market recognition of the name 'Tony Twist,' or in fact derived any benefit whatsoever."

Twist had contended that the character Antonio Twistelli, also known by the nickname Tony Twist, in the popular comic book series *Spawn* was unauthorized use of his name and hurt his endorsement possibilities. Judge Dierker said when McFarlane first used the name "Tony Twist," the plaintiff had no market recognition and "was earning precisely zero income from endorsements."

No action figures of the character were ever made. Of the 31,000 images that appeared in the Spawn series, Twist was included in just 166.

Ty's Surprise

The Beanie Babies world was turned upside down Jan. 8 when Ty announced its new reincarnation of plush for 2000 — Beanie Kids.

Late in 1999, Ty had announced the retirement of all Beanie Babies, prompting rumors that the company might halt production of the popular plush.

The announcement sparked a resurgence in retail sales, sending collectors scurrying to scoop up "the last of the Beanies." Ty even added fuel to the speculation by issuing a black bear called "The End."

But production didn't halt in 2000; Beanie Babies continued to be made, with the reincarnation of the plush animals into childlike Beanie Kids.

Third-party Grading in Toys

Coin collectors have it. So do comics and sports card fans. In 2000, several toy dealers started what is known in hobby circles as "third-party grading."

A neutral, but knowledgeable, dealer is paid to assess and grade the condition of an item. The item is then sealed in a package which cannot be opened without damaging the seal, often voiding the grade the toy was originally given.

In the toy industry, action figures and die-cast cars were the first to be affected by the practice.

How does it affect the hobby? A professional grader makes money, a collector gets an indisputable (supposedly) grade on his/her toy and a potential buyer gets an assurance of an accurate grading of a toy's condition.

Online Forces Team Up

Two leading Internet retailers, Amazon.com and Toysrus.com, joined up to offer consumers a co-branded toy and video game store. They hoped to have a site running in fall 2000.

Under the agreement, effective for 10 years, Amazon.com and Toysrus.com will each handle certain areas of the online store. Toysrus.com will handle the inventory with Amazon.com taking over site development, order fulfillments, customer service and storage of inventory.

"Mobilia" Magazine Folds

In April, *Mobilia* magazine announced that it would cease publication of its print magazine to focus on the growth of its Web site, *www.mobilia.com*.

Krause Publications purchased the active subscriber list and fulfilled outstanding subscriptions to *Mobilia*.

Changes in KP Magazines

In other Krause Publications developments, the three-year-old magazine *Toy Cars & Vehicles* changed its name to *Toy Cars & Models* to better reflect the magazine's focus and coverage.

In late 2000, Krause also ceased publication of *eBay Magazine*, founded in 1999 through a licensing agreement with the online auction giant eBay.

Tragedy Touches Toyland
'Toy Shop' Loses Beloved Writer

In our own bit of somber industry news, Krause Publications mourned the loss of book editor and *Toy Shop* columnist Jon Brecka.

Brecka, who wrote *Toy Shop*'s Hot Wheels column for the past several years, died Feb. 13, 2000, after injuries suffered in a Dec. 23, 1999, auto accident.

Brecka's ceaseless knowledge of Hot Wheels and his accurate reporting was known in the industry among collectors, dealers and manufacturers.

Before his death, while Brecka remained in a coma, cash and toy donations from Mattel, Playing Mantis, collectors and dealers helped a fund-raising effort to assist Brecka's wife, Shawn, and young daughter, Kendra.

Market Update
A Look at the 2000 Secondary Toy Market

By Angelo Van Bogart

Did you buy a Wonder Woman Barbie this year? A Hot Wheels Treasure Hunt car?

You weren't alone. These two toys were among many that commanded the attention of collectors this past year.

Oh, don't worry. Vintage dolls, die-cast and other toys are still out there, and still faring well, often thanks to the impact of the Internet.

But as competition increases, so do the choices for today's collectors.

Here's a quick look at how toys in your favorite categories fared in 2000.

Top 10 price lists taken from Krause Publications' *2001 Toys & Prices*.

Action Figures

Now is a great time to be a collector of 12-inch action figures. Hasbro's G.I. Joe has seen recent competition by companies such as 21st Century Toys and Dragon.

Each manufacturer is offering their figures in World War II gear, and the soldiers are finding new homes with collectors seeking a world a little outside Joe's realm.

"World War II is super hot," said Ed Harsh, who runs Hero Central in Reno, N.V.

"Modern stuff like special forces and SWAT is popular but not as popular as the World War II stuff," he added.

Not only are the major companies offering WWII items, but custom companies are making previously unavailable uniforms available to collectors.

"Dragon stuff is hot, and limited editions will be hot but not so much exclusives," Harsh said.

Those exclusives Harsh refers to are the Winter Gerhard figures offered by Dragon exclusively over the Internet. Many people without online access did not purchase them. That may have turned off completists who collected everything, and Harsh said many of them are more selective now about what they collect.

But the demand for that Internet exclusive figure is not necessarily gone.

"Winter Gerhard originally cost about $50, and it now goes for $100 to $150 online."

Collectors clamor for nearly all Dragon figures, so naturally one of the most sought-after figures is Hans, the first Dragon figure offered. Harsh reported an increase from $35 when new to $150 to $200 for the action figure.

Although they are quality products, figures from 21st Century Toys do not seem to be commanding more on the secondary market, according to Harsh.

Military figures by 21st Century Toys, like this U.S. Modern Infantry soldier, found collector interest this year, taking some business away from Hasbro's iconic G.I. Joe.

The Top 10 G.I. Joe Figures / Sets (in Mint in Package condition)

1. Foreign Soldiers of the World, Action Soldiers of the World, 1968 . . $5,000
2. G.I. Nurse, Action Girl Series, 1967 . . . . $4,000
3. Canadian Mountie Set, Action Soldier Series, 1967 . . . . $4,000
4. Dress Parade Adventure Pack, Action Soldier Series, 1968 . . . . $3,500
5. Crash Crew Fire Truck Set, Action Pilot Series, 1967 . . . . $3,500
6. Talking Landing Signal Officer Set, Action Sailor Series, 1968 . . . . $3,500
7. Talking Shore Patrol Set, Action Sailor Series, 1968 . . . . $3,500
8. Adventure Pack, Army Bivouac Series, Action Soldier Series, 1968 . $3,500
9. Military Police Uniform Set, Action Soldier Series, 1967 . . . . $3,500
10. Shore Patrol, Action Sailor Series, 1967 . . . . $3,500

"For some reason, they (21st Century) do some strange discounting," Harsh said. "People think they can get them for less on the secondary market."

Harsh said collectors may be waiting for the figures to be discounted before they buy them.

Action figure columnist John Marshall sees 21st Century figures differently.

"[Toys by] 21st Century are good investment pieces," Marshall notes. "You don't know if you will ever see an example of [a particular figure] again."

Marshall said that when 21st Century figures hit the shelves, they disappear within a week. Adding to their popularity, Marshall said, is that the company does not make "hundreds of thousands of each figure."

Harsh said vintage G.I. Joe items remain solid collector favorites, and he sees their prices holding steady in the future.

"Vintage G.I. Joe is holding steady, although there are no gains like in previous years," he added.

But even those popular Joes of yesteryear are facing competition.

"A lot of people who once collected vintage G. I. Joe look at their stuff and say it is obsolete because the new stuff is so detailed," Harsh said.

Although Marshall views the military action figure market as being strong, he said superheroes are following a trend of weak sales and interest in the market, but only for a short period.

"Superhero toys are just not getting the kind of money they would normally get," he said. "I think it is only temporary."

Toy dealer Bill Campbell has also noticed a leveling in the superhero playing field.

"Green Hornet and Batman have leveled out," he said. "But other superhero stuff is gradually moving up.

"[The] Shadow is still doing really well, and there is good interest in Captain America."

With last summer's film *X-Men*, and Batman and Spider-Man movies in the works, Marshall thinks the market will rejuvenate for these figures.

"I think superheroes will be back in vogue in a year or two," Marshall said, ending their two- to three-year slump.

Character Toys

So, if it's not the year of the superhero, which characters flipped collectors' lids?

Campbell said boxed watches of characters such as Wonder Woman and Felix the Cat have been popular. Campbell also said 1950s TV characters Beany and Cecil have seen a resurgence.

The Top 10 Action Figures
(excluding Captain Action, in Mint in Box condition)

1. Batgirl, Comic Heroine Posin' Dolls, Ideal, 1967 ....$4,500
2. Wonder Woman, Comic Heroine Posin' Dolls, Ideal, 1967 ....$3,000
3. Supergirl, Comic Heroine Posin' Dolls, Ideal, 1967 ....$3,000
4. Mera, Comic Heroine Posin' Dolls, Ideal, 1967 ....$3,000
5. Scorpio, Major Matt Mason, Mattel, 1967-70 ....$2,250
6. Batman's Wayne Foundation Penthouse, 1977,
    fiberboard, World's Greatest Super Heroes, Mego, 1972-78 ..$1,200
7. Mission Team Four-Pack, Major Matt Mason, Mattel, 1967-70, .$625
8. Romulan, Star Trek, Mego, 1976 ....$600
9. Callisto, Major Matt Mason, Mattel, 1967-70 ....$600
10. Mad Monster Castle, vinyl, Mad Monster Series, Mego $600

Some dealers report success with toys based on characters such as Felix the Cat.

The Top 10 Character Collectibles
(in Mint condition)

1. Action Comics #1, DC Comics, 1938, first appearance
    of Superman $185,000
2. Superman Member Ring, 1940 ....$70,000
3. Superman Gum Ring, Gum, Inc., 1940 ....$30,000
4. Little Orphan Annie Altascope Ring, Quaker, 1942 ....$25,000
5. Superman Candy Ring, Leader Novelty Candy, 1940 ......$20,000
6. Donald Duck Bicycle, Shelby, 1949 ....$10,000
7. Superman-Tim Club Ring, 1940s $10,000
8. Superman Trading Cards, Gum, Inc., 1940 ....$10,000
9. Batman Play Set, Ideal, 1966 ....$10,000
10. Superman Patch, 1939 ....$9,000

"The business [selling character toys] is very healthy and growing, and a lot of younger people are entering it (the hobby)," Campbell said. "There is always a strong market for rare items in extremely good condition."

Campbell credited toys such as Universal Monsters for keeping the collectors interested.

"Last year, Universal Monsters (from the 1960s) used to sell upward of $100," he said. "Now I am selling them for $125."

Felix the Cat is an unlikely contender to Universal Monsters, but collectors are just as interested, Campbell said.

"I buy 10 Felix items, and they are gone in two weeks," he said. "I just don't have anything that is dead; there has been continuing interest across the board."

What's not hot?

Mike Mitros of M & J Variety in New Jersey, who regularly sells character toys from Felix to *Tim Burton's Nightmare Before Christmas*, said Dilbert toys are slow movers.

"We cannot give Dilbert stuff away," he said, adding that WCW toys have fallen out of favor as well.

"WCW took a nose dive; it has totally died," Mitros said. "But WWF stuff is still strong."

Mitros noted that although the values of *Nightmare Before Christmas* items have dropped, they are selling better than ever.

"*Nightmare before Christmas* is still really strong," he said. "A lot of new stuff is being released." Late in 2000, the Tim Burton film was re-released in theaters.

"Applause did a set of roll-along figures for *Nightmare Before Christmas*, and there were loads of them on the market," Mitros said. "There was so much available, at one point you could buy them for a couple of dollars a piece. Now they are going for $30 a set."

Hot Wheels

Not every Hot Wheels car, with or without redline wheels, will fetch over $70,000 like the rear-loading surfboard Beach Bomb prototype that sold earlier in 2000.

But they may still fetch good prices. Ricky Smith of Old Tyme Toy Store reported that sales of redline Hot Wheels continued to be strong, with examples like the Olds 442 and the Classic Cord being among the most requested of the redlines.

Proving that Hot Wheels do not have to be vintage to be

Mattel's vintage redline Beatnik Bandit is a perennial favorite with Hot Wheels collectors.

The Top 10 Vintage Hot Wheels
(in Mint in Package condition)

1. Volkswagen Beach Bomb, surf boards in rear window, 1969 . . . .$7,000
2. Custom Camaro, 1968, white enamel $2,500
3. Snake, 1973, white/yellow $1,500
4. Mongoose, 1973, red/blue $1,400
5. Carabo, 1974, yellow $1,400
6. Baja Bruiser, light green, 1976 . . . .$1,300
7. Baja Bruiser, yellow, magenta in tampo, 1974 . . . .$1,200
8. Mustang Stocker, 1975, white $1,200
9. Custom Mustang, 1968 . . . .$1,200
10. Mercedes C-111, 1973 . . . .$1,200

The Top 10 Hot Wheels Numbered Packs
(in Mint in Package condition)

1. No. 51 '40s Woodie $700
2. No. 355 '67 Camaro, 1995 Treasure Hunt Series $600
3. No. 714 Talbot Lago $350
4. No. 672 #35-Dodge Concept Car, 1998 First Editions $350
5. No. 12 Jeep $275
6. No. 50 Rolls-Royce Phantom II $250
7. No. 271 Side Splitter $250
8. No. 88 Thunderbird Stocker $250
9. No. 89 Mini Truck $250
10. No. 75 Pontiac Banshee $200

Sometimes hot, sometimes not. Mattel's holiday issue Hot Wheels are often clearanced at stores but still desired by some completist collectors.

desirable, Smith noted that sales of modern limited editions have been strong, as have sale of some blackwalls.

"Loose limited editions and blackwalls do better than packaged because they are cheaper," Smith said.

Smith's sales of packaged blackwalls and newer Treasure Hunt cars have also been strong.

Toy Shop's Hot Wheels columnist Paul Provencher believes that redline and early 1970s Hot Wheels will continue to increase in value. But he sees the values of newer Hot Wheels headed in a different direction.

"People who are staying with the hobby are waiting to see items hit the shelves of their own hometowns" instead of buying online, Provencher said.

He also noted demand for blackwall cars of the late 1970s and 1980s will stabilize in the near future.

"Old collectors already have these cars, and new collectors don't seem to be interested," Provencher said.

When asked about the new trend of customizing Hot Wheels and its impact on collectibility, Provencher noted that cars done by reputable customizers with a familiar name may become collectible, but those done by novice customizers will not affect future value.

What's faring best? "Harder-to-find redlines seem to have increased," he said, adding that "Variations seem to be realizing higher prices."

Barbie

The Barbie market is sending out mixed signals among both retailers and secondary market dealers. What they both agree on is that vintage Mint in Box dolls are the strongest-selling dolls in the market.

"I think early Mint in Box dolls have been very hot," said Sandy Holder of The Doll Attic.

"I sold a [Ponytail] #1 at auction that was Mint in Box, and it went over $15,000," she said. Another Ponytail #1 brunette sold for $8,700 at a McMaster's auction in 2000.

Mike Tickal of Your Old Friends Doll Shop agreed that quality, vintage dolls are still popular among collectors.

"Quality stuff sells, but common dolls sell poorly," Tickal said.

Both Holder and Tickal find collectors interested in Mattel's new "silkstone" line of dolls and the accompanying lingerie fashions.

"The fashions for silkstones have been very hot in the collector line," Holder noted, adding that she has been consistently busy filling customer requests all year.

"In new dolls, nothing is hot," Tickal said. "The whole market is down."

While Tickal sees most of the common items going down in value, he noted that new items do sell extremely well immediately after release, but after the initial boom, dolls don't move quite as quickly.

Holder was only able to identify two slow sellers this year in the Barbie line which may surprise

The Top 10 Barbie Dolls (in Mint in Box condition)

1. Ponytail Barbie #1, brunette, 1959 . . . .$8,000
2. Ponytail Barbie #1, blond, 1959 . . . .$7,500
3. Ponytail Barbie #2, brunette, 1959 . . . .$6,650
4. Ponytail Barbie #2, blond, 1959 . . . .$6,350
5. American Girl Side-Part Barbie, brunette, blond, titian, 1965 . .$3,875
6. Color Magic Barbie, midnight hair, 1966 . . . .$3,200
7. Midge's Ensemble Gift Set, 1964 . . . .$3,150
8. Barbie's Round the Clock Gift Set, Bubblecut, 1964 . . . .$3,000
9. Barbie Beautiful Blues Gift Set, 1967 . . . .$3,000
10. Fashion Queen Barbie & Ken Trousseau Gift Set, 1964 . . . . .$2,800

Vintage Barbie dolls, like these shown, maintain their popularity and values each year. Photo courtesy of Mattel.

collectors. Two character dolls did not sell as well as anticipated.

"I don't think the Elvis doll was as popular as we thought it would be," she said. "Dorothy (from *The Wizard of Oz*) was not a popular seller either."

Tickal found that many crossover items — those that appeal to not only Barbie collectors — have done well.

"All of the crossover stuff is, and will, do well," Tickal said, referring to last year's best-sellers Coca-Cola Barbie and Harley-Davidson Barbie and Ken.

Tickal cited an evolution in his customer base to explain the change in the Barbie market.

"The speculators are gone, and I'm [now] selling to collectors," he said.

Western Toys

Robert Donovan of Donovan's Western Toys has sold Western toys for 12 years. He's seen items like a cowboy coloring book that once commanded $75 now sell for $30. He has also seen customers' expectations get higher.

"People expect Mint in Box when before they were happy to get just the toy," Donovan said.

Other items that Donovan has seen diminish in value are Hopalong Cassidy cups.

"They used to start at $35, and I recently sold one for $19.95," he said.

Although some prices have suffered, many other items remain popular with collectors, and Donovan has recently noticed a younger crowd entering the field.

"What has blossomed now are Mattel's Shootin' Shell guns," he said, adding that they are proving popular with collectors who grew up in the early 1980s.

And even despite the growing political incorrectness of toy guns, Donovan still sells them for top prices. He even joked that he often sells a toy gun for more than others might get for real guns. But Donovan warned collectors to be vigilant of reproductions on the market.

"Don't pay a premium for a piece that has repro parts; almost all cap guns can have repro parts," Donovan warned.

Other Western characters that have thrived under the pressure of online sales include *The Rifleman*, Paladin (*Have Gun, Will Travel*) and Annie Oakley items. Fewer of these items were made compared with toys based on the "big four," Gene Autry, Roy Rogers, Hopalong Cassidy and the Lone Ranger.

But in addition to the big four, Donovan noted consistent demand for cowgirl items.

The Top 10 Western Toys (in Mint condition)

1. Hopalong Cassidy Roller Skates, Rollfast $1,000
2. Hopalong Cassidy Radio, Arvin, 1950s $600
3. Hopalong Cassidy Cap Gun, Wyandotte, 1950s $600
4. Roy Rogers Toy Chest, 1950s $550
5. Buck Jones Rangers Cowboy Suit, Yankiboy, 1930s $500
6. Hopalong Cassidy Western Series, Timpo, 1950s $475
7. Lone Ranger Record Player, Dekka, 1940s $450
8. Roy Rogers Play Set, Amsco, 1950s $440
9. Roy Rogers Alarm Clock, Ingraham, 1950s $440
10. Tom Mix Big Little Book Picture Puzzles, 1930s $425

Items depicting Roy Rogers, or one of the other well-known cowboy legends, consistently attract buyers, although prices may be softening on some vintage items.

The Top 10 Lunch Boxes (in Near Mint condition)

1. 240 Robert, steel, Aladdin, 1978 ....$2,500
2. Toppie Elephant, steel, American Thermos, 1957 ....$1,600
3. Home Town Airport Dome, steel, King Seeley, 1960 ....$1,000
4. Underdog, steel, Okay Industries, 1974 ....$900
5. Knight in Armor, steel, Universal, 1959 ....$ 825
6. Ballerina, vinyl, Universal, 1960s $800
7. Superman, steel, Universal, 1954 ....$800
8. Dudley Do-Right, steel, Universal, 1962 ....$800
9. Bullwinkle & Rocky, steel, Universal, 1962 ....$800
10. Little Friends, vinyl, Aladdin, 1982 ....$760

Advertising Toys

Does Count Chocula ring a bell? How about Frankenberry? The General Mills cereal monsters, remembered by many advertising toy collectors, are among the most popular figures at M & J Variety.

"I did real well with Wacky Wobblers [bobbin' head figures] of Count Chocula, Boo-Berry and Frankenberry, as well as Cracker Jack," Mitros said.

Mitros said there were three characters that found renewed interest this year — the buxom

Betty Boop, the bashful Popeye and the 85th-anniversary Raggedy Ann.

Restaurant king Big Boy also found significant interest, although Mitros said the advertising icon has always lived large in collectors' minds.

"Big Boy always had a real strong Japanese following, and he also has a real strong following out West and down South," he said.

Mitros said collectors are more interested in finding three-dimensional representations of the advertising characters, rather than depictions of them on mugs or on paper items.

"Statutes and three-dimensional figures always do better, but there are collectors who collect everything on that character," he said.

Like so many other toys, advertising and character toys that were once difficult to find have become easier to locate in online auctions. As a result, Mitros said there are more bargains available.

"The Internet has been ferretting out people's attics," he said.

Also like other collectibles, Mitros said that advertising toys in poorer condition have lost value as the market has become flooded.

Angelo Van Bogart was Krause Publications' toy department editorial intern for summer 2000.

For more information or to order "2001 Toys & Prices," call Krause Publications at (800) 258-0929.

"2001 Toys & Prices" includes prices for more than 20,000 toys.

The re-release of "Tim Burton's Nightmare Before Christmas" created renewed interest — and new collectibles — commemorating the film's spooky characters like Lock, Shock and Barrel, pictured above.

The Top 10 Advertising Toys
(in Mint condition)

1. Quisp Bank, Quaker Oats, 1960s $850
2. Reddy Kilowatt Bobbin' Head, Reddy Comm., 1960s $450
3. Mr. Peanut Figure, Planters Peanuts, 1930s $375
4. Esky Store Display, *Esquire* Magazine, 1940s $375
5. Elsie the Cow Cookie Jar, Borden's, 1950s $350
6. Speedy Figure, Alka-Seltzer, 1963 .... $350
7. Vegetable Man Display, Kraft, 1980 .... $275
8. Barnum's Animal Crackers Cookie Jar, Nabisco, 1972 ...... $275
9. Vegetable Man Bank, Kraft, 1970s $275
10. Clark Bar Figure, Beatrice Foods, 1960s $275

GOOD CLEAN FUN — Although not on our Top 10 list, Mr. Bubble remains a fun advertising character for collectors to hunt down.

Top 10 Boomer Toys
Did Your Favorites Make Our List?

By Angelo Van Bogart

PEZ. Slinky. Etch-A-Sketch. What are the greatest baby boomer toys of all time?

While everyone may have a sentimental favorite, some toys reign as memorable to many.

Author Mark Rich has researched and played with many favorites to write his book *100 Greatest Baby Boomer Toys* (Krause Publications, 2000).

Whether you agree or disagree with his list, it is difficult to resist the trip down memory lane.

The book includes 100 of the greatest; listed below are the top 10, in descending order. Enjoy.

No. 10 — Slinky

Children often make toys out of the most mundane objects, but the creator of the Slinky was no child. Richard James stumbled onto the concept for Slinky while he was designing a spring for a marine application. After knocking one of his springs over, James noticed that it would climb down a set of books . . . over and over. The spring quickly became a hit with his children and their friends.

Unable to sell the concept to a manufacturer, James made the toy on his own. He convinced Gimbel's department store to allow him to sell the toys in their stores from a display that he manned. James' toy was an instant success in the hands of children, and the Jameses found success with the toy for 50 years.

Where do Barbie and G.I. Joe fall on our list of the greatest baby boomer toys ever?

No. 9 — Hot Wheels

Redlines. Mighty stance. Powerful pipes dumping out from under the sides. Hot Wheels cars were meant for speed, and Mattel capitalized on that concept. With their California-beach looks and metalflake paint jobs, the cars overtook the market Matchbox had dominated for years before Hot Wheels debuted in the late 1960s.

The California-influenced cars did not carry the same level of accuracy as the competition but gained immense popularity through their ability to find speed on kitchen floors and sidewalks. Matchbox simply couldn't keep up on the tracks or the stores shelves.

Although a late baby boomer toy, these cars have remained popular with today's children and are destined to appear on other generations' top 10 lists.

No. 8 — Hula Hoop

Blame plastic. The creation of plastic spawned a world of toys previously unimaginable by allowing them to be safe and lightweight.

The Hula Hoop was the lightest of the plastic group, consisting of a skinny ring that churned around the waists of children like a tornado around a mobile home park.

A single loop created a huge, but brief, craze in the summer of 1958 that toy manufacturers were unable to

Mark Rich's book hails the greatest baby boomer toys of all time.

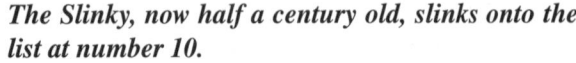
The Slinky, now half a century old, slinks onto the list at number 10.

keep up with. But just as quickly as it came, it disappeared.

No. 7 — Frisbee

A toy based on a pie tin. Who could have known that a simple piece of tin could create so many hours of fun for so many people?

Yale students threw pie pans from Frisbie's Pie Co., a local bakery, as a source of recreation. It may have also satisfied the need for college-aged men to throw everything in sight and within reach. The students would yell "Fris-bie" to alert people around them that the tin was airborne.

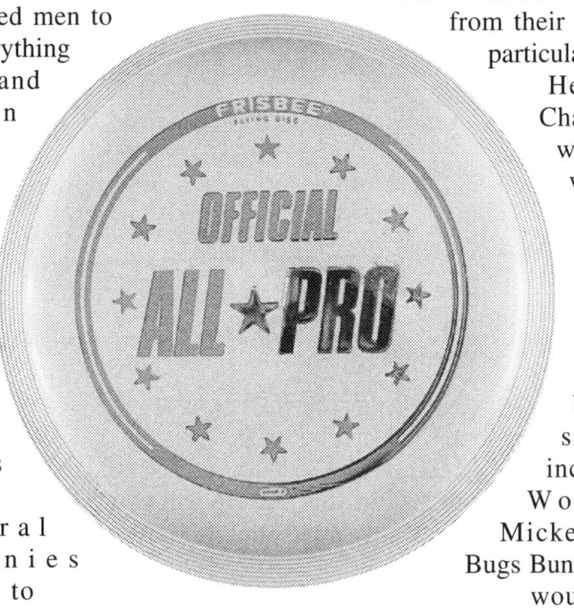

Several companies attempted to mass produce and market plastic versions of the toy, but none were successful until Wham-O renamed the disc "Frisbee" and trademarked the name. And it has stuck in the minds, but not the hands, of Americans ever since.

Frisbee's beginnings originated with a pie plate. The evergreen toy ranked No. 7 on our list.

No. 6 — Kenner Easy-Bake Oven

A pair of light bulbs, a package of Betty Crocker cake mix and a lack of adult supervision spelled fun for many small children who couldn't wait to master the kitchen.

Kenner's Easy-Bake Oven came to children in turquoise-colored plastic and promised that their cakes would be "just like mom's."

Not the first children's oven on the shelves of toy stores, Easy-Bake was the first to use the heat solely from light bulbs to bake the cake and cookie mixes supplied through Betty Crocker.

Easy-Bake was a popular name on the mouths of children at the time, and it undoubtly showed up on their holiday wish lists.

Still available today, the Easy-Bake now looks more like a modern microwave oven but operates on the same principle.

No. 5 — Chatty Cathy and Friends

The parents of boomer children were treated to a new sound from their children's toys, particularly toy dolls.

Her name was Chatty Cathy, and when her string was pulled, she spoke through a voice box from within her body. Mattel later put the voice box into television characters including Woody Woodpecker, Mickey Mouse and Bugs Bunny. Even Barbie would get a voice box by the late 1960s, proving how popular the single box had become in the world of toys.

No. 4 — Matchbox

In the early 1950s, America was on the move, and so were its children. By introducing the tiny and portable Matchbox vehicle that could fit in their pocket, England's Lesney created a product that children could bring anywhere for entertainment.

The tiny cars were accurate representations of automobiles on the road and displayed a level of detail not commonly found on other cars of its small scale.

Hubley and

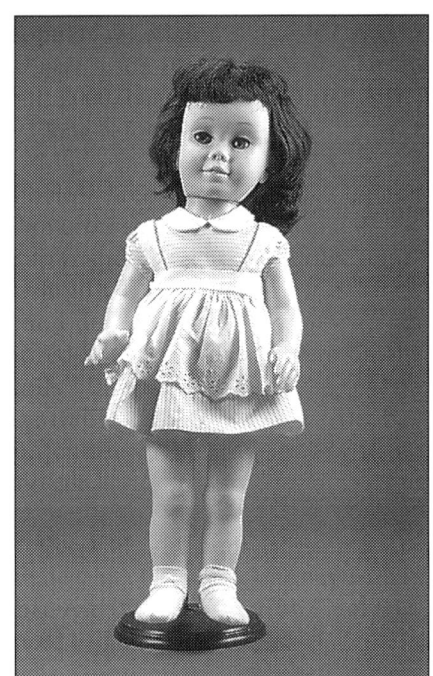

A talking doll, like the Chatty Cathy pictured, was quite a development in baby boomer toys.

Tootsietoy followed their lead and produced cars in the Matchbox tradition, but few were able to match their success. In sandbox circles, the name had stuck — all of the imitations were now called Matchbox, at least until a hot new car wheeled into town from Mattel.

No. 3 — G.I. Joe

He had the best of timing and the worst of timing. He was able to jump through a brief window in time and gain success on the shelves and acceptance among the masses. He was, and will forever be, Hasbro's G.I. Joe.

He went against the long-held

Pictured is a later reincarnation of the classic Easy-Bake Oven by Kenner. The creative toy is still marketed today.

Toy Shop Annual 2001

belief that boys were not to play with anything that could be construed as a doll, for fear of humiliation.

With the successful introduction of Barbie only five years earlier, Hasbro introduced G.I. Joe in 1964 to the children of World War II veterans. He had full military attire to help him gain the approval of parents, but more importantly, the toy allowed children to role play with an adult figure. The action figure became successful immediately, but the climate in the military quickly began to change only a few years later and it became obvious that Joe would have to change with it.

As facts about the Vietnam War became more apparent in the American psyche, Joe toned down his war theme and became an action man — Adventure Team Joe. The personality overhaul couldn't return him to his former glory, and his popularity waned in his original 12-inch form.

No. 2 — Mr. Potato Head

The second best toy of the baby boomer generation is a food-based toy. A spud.

With his plastic body parts, Mr. Potato Head gave permission to children to play with their food.

Children could take ears, eyes, noses and mouths and place them onto an actual vegetable by means of spikes in the backs of the plastic sensory organs. After completing its face arrangement, the vegetable was stuck onto the top of a plastic body and he was ready for play. One can only imagine the mutilated examples of vegetables as children continually changed the positions of Mr. Potato Head's facial parts.

Mr. Potato Head started his rise to the top as a cereal premium in the early 1950s before his creator, George Lerner, sold the idea to the then-stationery company Hasbro.

Mr. Potato Head fit the definition of the baby boomer toy as well as any

Bumped out of the top position by a slender doll, Mr. Potato Head commands a strong second place on our list.

other. Aside from allowing creativity in children, Mr. Potato Head was among the first entirely-new toys seen after World War II, and his use of plastic would show the direction for other toys to follow. He was first seen in *Life* magazine by parents and on television for children, but not just any television show, *The Jackie Gleason Show*. In fact, this spud was the first toy to be advertised on television (1952).

Mr. Potato Head held a long reign in toyland and eventually succumbed to plastic surgery when he was given a facelift. His perishable head became plastic, and his head and body melded into one large potato-shaped body.

His popularity never suffered for it.

No. 1 — Barbie

The queen still rules among children, both past and present.

But it almost wasn't that way.

While Ruth Handler watched her daughter and friends play with paper dolls, she noticed that the children preferred playing with the adult paper dolls and role-playing with them rather than the baby paper dolls.

The observation set in motion ideas that broke conventional wisdom of the time. Had someone outside of the circles of the toy companies noticed and went to the toy companies, would Barbie have been created? Doubtful, since Handler had the means to bring the doll to the market. You see, Handler and her husband ran Mattel, and after convincing her husband that an adult doll was what children really wanted, she targeted retailers at the 1959 New York Toy Fair. Using their brand name, Mattel was able to sell the new doll named after Ruth's daughter, Barbara.

The body used for Ruth's doll was based on a German comic strip character created in 1952. Lilli, the creation of cartoonist Reinhard Beuthien, became a three-dimensional figure with a slender body and heavy curves. Lilli's popularity in Germany eventually waned, and Mattel picked her up.

Like any good fashion model, Barbie started a trend, or at least latched onto one and helped to make it common — accessories. Many of Barbie's items were not necessary but rather for display and to play dress up. And it drew children to her.

What other toys made Rich's list? Some of the notables include Tonka trucks, Sun Rubber dolls, trolls, Gumby, Twister and Colorforms. For a closer, more colorful look at the greatest toys of the baby boomer era, check out Rich's book. To order, call Krause Publications at (800) 258-0929.

Hot Wheels have barely slowed down in popularity in more than 30 years.

24
Toy Shop Annual 2001

Make War, Make Money
Military Toys Prevail in 2000

War is hell.

But it can also mean a lot of money, especially at a time when military toys are selling stronger than usual, even in times of international unrest.

At the National Model and Hobby Show held in late 2000 in Chicago, a handful of companies displayed their new products. And while the show is generally a showcase for buyers of model railroads, die-cast models and radio-controlled toys, this year's show included many military-themed toys, especially action figures.

Hasbro, Blue Box, 21st Century Toys, Cotswold Collectibles and Dragon all had representatives on hand. Most of the representatives said they had not displayed at the show before but thought they'd increase their exposure through this annual event.

Surprisingly, Hasbro, which recently announced major office closures and layoffs, was in attendance, albeit with a tiny, almost hidden booth. In their first year at the show, the company displayed current G.I. Joe product, including the much-anticipated John F. Kennedy figure, featuring JFK from his World War II days. Other military figures on display included the Navy Gunner and Navajo Code Talker.

The company's new line of higher-end porcelain figurines featuring military scenes were also on display.

The Ultimate Soldier, 21st Century

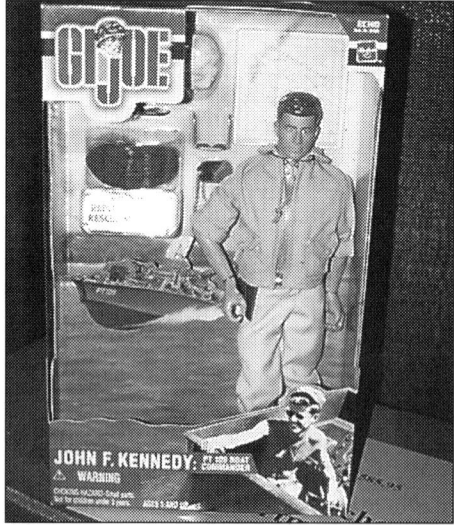

Hasbro's JFK G.I. Joe was one highlight of 2000.

Who's Making the Military?

Want more information on the military toys mentioned in this article? Here are the Web sites of the manufacturers listed.

Hasbro
www.hasbrocollectors.com

Blue Box
www.blueboxtoys.com

Cotswold Collectibles
www.elitebrigade.com

21st Century Toys
www.21stcenturytoys.com

Playing Mantis
www.playingmantis.com

Corgi
www.corgiclassics.com

Maisto
www.maisto.com

Ertl Collectibles/Britains
www.wbritain.com

Toys' answer to G.I. Joe, stormed into the show with a bigger booth, right around the corner from Hasbro. Their detailed WWII soldiers were poised atop tanks and vehicles scaled to their size.

The Elite Brigade, specialty figures presented by Cotswold Collectibles, were in force as well. New figures included a German Afrika Korps Tropical Gerbirgs-jager. The figure represents the battle of Kasserine Pass between U.S. and German forces in WWII. In addition to displaying its other custom figures — like German SS guards and Japanese Infantry soldiers — Cotswold introduced a Santa suit for G.I. Joe and similarly-scaled figures.

Playing Mantis, taking its cue from a popular video game, is creating military figures targeted at a younger audience with its Army Men line. These "little green army men" figures are 7 inches tall and feature weapons and accessories.

Ertl Collectibles' line of William Britain toy soldiers continues its detailed line with new pieces re-enacting the battles of the American Revolution, including a figure of Paul Revere on horseback. Figures from the American Civil War and Napoleonic Wars will also be available.

A Battery of Die-Cast

Waging war in the toy industry isn't just a battle royal among action figures. Die-cast manufacturers are on the front lines as well.

Capitalizing on the strength of Hasbro's G.I Joe license, Maisto is introducing small-scale die-cast military vehicles, including a helicopter, trucks, dozers and tanks. The vehicles are packaged on a cardback with the G.I. Joe logo.

One of the most polished and touching military offerings next year comes from Britain's Corgi.

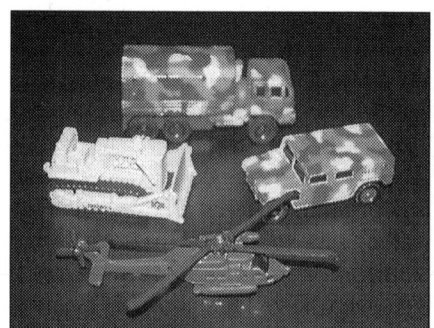

Pictured are four vehicles in Maisto's licensed G.I. Joe die-cast line.

The new Unsung Heroes lineup honors America's Vietnam veterans.

"While interviewing these men, I learned how brave, committed and patriotic they all were. These are the true unsung heroes," said Corgi's Director of Marketing Richard Walker.

The collection includes four vehicles, slated for a fall 2000 release. U.S. Marine Corps vehicles include an M48 A3 Patton tank and an M151 A1 Mutt utility truck. U.S. Army vehicles include a UH-1C Huey Hog Helicopter Gunship and a M35 A1 "Deuce and a half" 2.5-ton truck. Each vehicles comes with a certificate and booklet detailing the vehicle's specifications and the story of a soldier who operated the vehicle.

These personal accounts bring the war home for collectors. Rather than just more die-cast vehicles, these vehicles become "something far more meaningful, a glipse and reminder into what life was like for soldiers in Vietnam," said John Dunkel, Corgi vice president and former U.S. Marine, Danang 1970.

'Honey, I Shrunk the G.I. Joe'

America's favorite Man of Action just got a little smaller.

Hasbro has licensed its popular core product — G.I. Joe — to several companies who will make smaller-scale collectibles based on the action figure. Early prototypes were displayed in late 2000 at the National Model and Hobby Show in Chicago.

Leading the charge is William Britain (part of the Ertl Collectibles line). On display were their 54mm pewter figures which replicate figures in the Action Marine, Action Pilot, Action Soldier and Action Sailor lines.

The attractively boxed sets include three uniformed figures and a miniature replica of the original G.I. Joe boxes. Each three-piece set will retail in specialty stores for around $60. For more information, visit www.wbritain.com.

Maisto will produce small-scale vehicles under the G.I. Joe banner. Included in the line are a helicopter, trucks, dozers and tanks.

Hasbro itself will enter a new arena this year with higher-end porcelain figurines based on G.I. Joe themes.

Pictured at right are three small-scale (54mm) pewter G.I. Joe figures in William Britain's new line. Three-piece sets will come packaged with a miniature replica of the original Hasbro G.I. Joe box.

Military Toys: Tribute or Violence Revisited?

At the National Model and Hobby Show in Chicago in late 2000, a kind gentleman stopped at my booth to lament the current influx of military toys into the retail market.

A veteran, the man was displeased with the amount of action figures depicting soldiers, especially notorious war criminals and World War II axis soldiers. He served in the military and was offended that so many companies were offering toys that "glorified war."

While I agreed that there were numerous companies making these products, I disagreed that the toys (well, most of them anyway) glorified war.

Conversely, I felt many of the companies were making toys and collectibles as tributes to our veterans and war heroes.

Two recent examples include Hasbro's accessory-filled John F. Kennedy G.I. Joe and Corgi's Unsung Heroes line, which honors America's Vietnam War veterans. Corgi's line even includes tribute pamphlets with actual stories of Vietnam soldiers.

Many of the companies making these toys do so after receiving numerous requests from collectors. Many veterans and history buffs are looking for items to add to their collections. For them, I assume, it is a way of looking back with honor on battles well-fought for a cause they believed in.

It's not hard to defend these "toys;" they are clearly made as adult collectibles. They are not packaged, priced or marketed toward children.

It may be harder to defend recent figures made of notorious figures such as Adolf Hitler or the German SS soldiers. But you don't have to agree with what the figure represents to recognize it as a historically-accurate piece. And the manufacturers, I believe, are attempting to fill gaps left by the major manufacturers, who won't — or choose not to — touch the controversial subject matter.

Opposing views on these toys will exist just as opposing political views on war continue to exist. But I appreciate the gentleman stopping by my booth to voice his opinion. It helped me understand another point of view on this controversial subject and allowed me to look at these "toys" in another way.

Sharon Korbeck
korbecks@krause.com

Auction Action

Mickey Wind-ups, Rare Robot Collection Headline Year 2000

By Angelo Van Bogart and Tom Bartsch

Lots of action, rare toys and unexpected bids are characteristics of toy auctions. It's the one place people can remain anonymous while paying big bucks for a rare, vintage toy or one that simply recalls memories of their childhood.

It's also a place where toys of the past can take on a new life, reaching values never dreamed of when they first hit store shelves decades ago. Auctions also reflect the true demand for the toys presented, setting trends for future sales.

The following show some of these characteristics for the year 2000.

Here's what toys sold for at auction in their respective categories, giving a glimpse into their future worth should they hit the auction block again.

Guntherman's four-seat tourer with chauffer and two passengers sold for $30,800 (twice its presale estimate) at a Bertoia auction.

Ultra Rare Robot Collection Considered 'Best Ever' at Sotheby's

This year's auction action was hotter than ever, with many surprising bids popping up. Unfortunately, one of the highlights of the year will occur after this publication goes to press.

The legendary collection of robots and space toys belonging to the late F.H. Griffith was auctioned off by Sotheby's New York in December.

Griffith was considered the first American robot collector, buying the futuristic toys when they were available at retail. Though he was modest to his collection's contents, the whole world gave its approval.

Some of the highlights of the collection include a Diamond Planet robot (presale estimate $30,000 to $40,000), a complete Gang of Five (including Machine Man, $40,000 to $60,000) and a battery-operated Mego Man thought to be the only example in existence ($50,000 to $70,000).

Other 20th-century robots include lead-armed version Atomic Robot Man ($1,000 to $1,400) and Lilliput ($5,000 to $7,000).

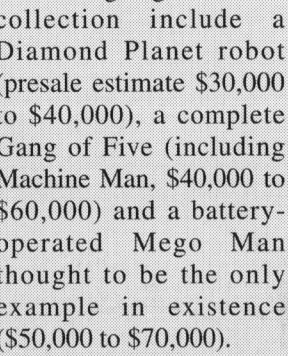

The boxed Diamond Planet Robot. Photo courtesy of Sotheby's.

Vehicle Toys

Die-cast vehicles are one of the hottest properties right now, both on store shelves and at auction. It seems to be one of the few toy categories currently on the upswing.

However, things might be in for a change with the introduction of third-party grading. Grading could have a big impact on future auction prices, like it has in the sports card and coin hobbies, should it take hold. It will be interesting to see how things unfold next year as the practice establishes more of a presence.

That said, here's how some die-cast

Though pedal cars weren't plentiful at auction in 2000, this Buick pedal car sold for $9,200 at a Skinner Auction. The pedal car was a 38-inch Steelcraft Buick.

Toy Shop Annual 2001

The rare, vintage plane is an early version of the Wright Brothers airplane. An Ernst Plank masterpiece, it sold for $35,200 at a Bertoia auction.

vehicles fared this year at auction.

At a Lloyd Ralston auction early in 2000, a set of three Corgi vehicles in Mint and Excellent condition sold for $2,150. The set included a 466 Commer milk float, a 1151 Scammel semi-trailer and a 462 Commer van. The sale also featured an illuminated Corgi Toys sign which brought $1,000.

Other Corgi best sellers included a Mini Mostest Pop Art car ($1,400) and a Corgi James Bond Mustang ($270).

The auction was also strong in Dinky vehicles, including a Mobil gas tanker ($1,125), a RAC Patrol gift set ($930) and a Holland Coachcraft van ($1,600).

More leading prices for Dinky included a Dinky Guy van ($870), a Meccano delivery van ($670) and a Lyons Tea delivery van ($625).

Pedal cars were not plentiful at auction this year, but a Buick pedal car, modeled from a 1920s version, tripled its presale estimate when it realized $9,200 at a Skinner auction mid-way through the year.

Pressed steel also made a few appearances at Skinner auctions. A Buddy L tank line sprinkler truck sold for $1,380, and a Buddy L fire pumper brought $1,495.

Richard Opfer auctioned off an 18-1/2-inch Buddy L road roller for $2,420, despite it being a restored piece. Not finding nearly as high of a

Guide to Major Auction Houses

Here's addresses for the nation's leading auction houses:

- **Noel Barrett Antiques & Auctions**, Box 300, 6183 Carversville Rd., Carversville, PA 18913 (215) 297-5109
- **Bill Bertoia Auctions**, 1881 Spring Rd., Vineland, NJ 08361 (609) 692-1881
- **Butterfield & Butterfield**, 220 San Bruno Ave., San Francisco, CA 94103 (415) 861-7500, 7601 Sunset Blvd., Los Angeles, CA 90046 (323) 850-7500
- **Christie's**, 219 E. 67th St., New York, NY 10021 (212) 606-0645
- **Hake's Americana & Collectibles**, P.O. Box 1444, York, PA 17405-1444 (717) 848-1333
- **Henry/Peirce Auctioneers**, 1525 S. Arcadian Dr., New Berlin, WI 53151 (414) 797-7933
- **Randy Inman Auctions**, P.O. Box 726, Waterville, ME 04903 (207) 872-6900
- **James Julia Inc.**, P.O. Box 830, Fairfield, ME 04937 (207) 453-7125
- **Just Kids Nostalgia**, 310 New York Ave., Huntington, NY 11743 (516) 423-8449
- **Richard Opfer**, 1919 Green-Spring Dr., Timonium, MD 21093 (410) 252-5035
- **Skinner Inc.**, 357 Main St., Bolton, MA 01740 (978) 779-6241
- **Smith House Toys.**, P.O. Box 336, Eliot, MA 03903 (207) 439-4614
- **Sotheby's**, 1334 York Ave., New York, NY 10021 (212) 606-7176
- **Toy Scouts**, 137 Casterton Ave., Akron, OH 44303 (330) 836-0668
- **'Tiques**, RR1, Box 49B, Rte. 34, Old Bridge, NJ 08857 (732) 721-0221
- **TV Toyland**, 223 Wall St., Huntington, NY 11743 (516) 385-1306

This early tinplate clockwork motorcycle with a goggled driver sold for $20,900 at a Bertoia Auction.

price were two White vehicles — a steam shovel and a tanker truck. The 27-1/2-inch steam shovel reached $1,870, while the 26-inch tanker sold for $1,540.

Some high prices were realized at a Bill Bertoia auction, as bidding was fired up to $30,800 for a Guntherman four-seat open tourer that carried a chauffer and two passengers. At the same auction, a hand-painted Märklin fire pumper with spectactular detailing in Excellent condition sold for $35,200.

Tin vehicles found reasonable prices at an International Toy Collectors Association (ITCA) auction in 2000. A Bandai tin friction-powered 1956 Ford Ranch Wagon fetched $220, while a Linemar 1954 Chevrolet two-door sedan sold for $385.

An early version of the Wright Brothers' plane flew high at a Bertoia auction with a winning bid of $35,200. Made of tinplate, the toy was created by Ernst Plank.

Also at Bertoia, an early tinplate clockwork motorcycle closed out at $20,900. The bike included a goggled driver riding behind a brass headlamp.

Tipp & Co. toys were presented by Christie's. The friction-powered Mail Lorry sporting a lithographed exterior caught a winning bid of $1,030. Also present was a lithographed clockwork Tipper Wagon that sold for $410.

Christie's also offered a Corgi Gift Set 21 Chipperfields Circus Train with Scammell Handyman Cab and Menagerie Trailer. One collector snapped it up for $1,786. Also, a Schuco 2010 Magico Alfa Romeo in its original box sold for $1,692.

Tin offerings from an Opfer auction included a 3-inch tinplate open car with driver that fetched $550, as well as a delivery boy riding on a cycle cart which sold for $1,210.

Other automotive offerings included a 12-1/2-inch red Carette limousine with opening doors. It sold for $5,390. A 7-1/2-inch wind-up delivery truck bearing an advertisement for Hochschild Kohn department store in Baltimore carried bidding to $4,840.

Slot Cars

Slot cars do not appear frequently at auction, and when they did last year, they received mixed signals.

An Aurora store display poster from 1967 found an astonishing bid of $1,250 at a Toy Scouts auction. The piece of slot car art realized the lofty price partly due to the high level of quality in artwork on early Aurora packages and displays.

At a Lloyd Ralston auction, individual and multiple lots of Aurora Thunderjet and AFX slot cars all hovered near the $100 mark. A pair of 1963 Corvettes in Good condition sold for $90, while a Thunderjet Fairlane on a Vibrator chassis brought $100.

The auction also included a lot of five Aurora Cigar Box cars with two Willy's, a Ford GT, a Camaro and an Oldsmobile Toronado. The group sold for $100, while another individual Thunderjet, a Ford Torino, realized $120.

Cast Iron

Cast-iron toys include a wide selection, and the year 2000 was no different.

Bertoia auctions, known for their frequent sales of high-end cast-iron toys and doorstops, moved several cast-iron pieces in 2000.

In a fall auction, one cast-iron toy stood out. A Hubley 1927 Packard Straight Eight in Excellent condition sold for $20,000. The extremely rare piece was blue with a black roof and full running boards.

An early 1920s Chevy sedan with a rear spare brought $1,045, while a 1928 Arcade moving van with Lammert's Furniture & Draperies printed across its side found a new home for $2,310.

In the realm of cast-iron doorstops, an extremely rare Halloween Girl

This Halloween Girl doorstop, estimated at $3,000 to $3,500, brought $14,300 at Bertoia.

A cast-iron 1927 Packard Straight Eight, made by Hubley, brought $20,000 at a Bertoia auction. The piece was in Excellent condition.

sample in Excellent condition, sold for $14,300

A car featuring comic strip character Andy Gump brought $2,310. For toys that required a little bit of fuel, Bertoia's even offered a pair of miniature Arcade gas pumps that went for $660.

At Opfer, a 20-inch New York battleship sold for $1,375 and an 11-inch Kilgore TAT airplane sold for $1,595.

The Opfer auction also included a 9-inch Kenton touring sedan with passenger. It brought $1,265.

Banks

Vehicle toys weren't the only cast-iron venue for buyers in 2000. Banks cashed in at auction as well.

The desirable Darktown Battery mechanical bank hit the high mark at Opfer selling for $2,860. The bank is a favorite among collectors of both Black Americana as well as high-quality banks.

Other banks at Opfer included an Always Did 'Spise a Mule bank in Good to Very Good condition that realized $1,265, and a restored Uncle Sam bank that brought $1,375.

A cast-iron Punch and Judy mechanical bank showed up at an ITCA auction, selling for $3,300.

Ponytail Barbie #1 Commands $8,700

Barbie, namely the brunette Ponytail #1 with her original box, was not only the featured attraction at a McMasters auction that included more than 1,000 Barbie and friends dolls, but also became one of the most talked-about Barbies this year.

Bought as a birthday present, the Ponytail #1 sold for $8,700 despite a loose ponytail, discoloration and a stain on her toes. The box still had the original sticker price of $2.98, though it did show some wear.

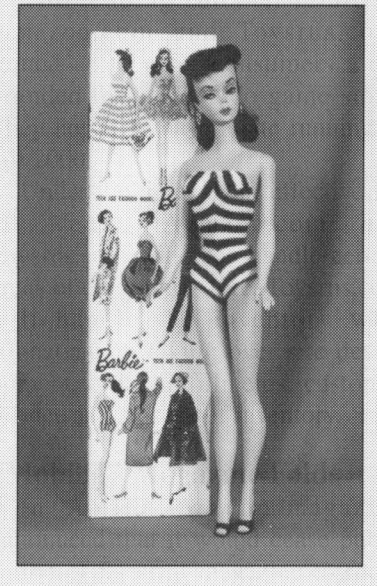

This Ponytail #1 brought $8,700 at a McMasters auction in 2000.

Several banks representing urban landmarks brought outstanding prices at a Bertoia auction, including a brass version of the Jarmulowski Building that rocketed up to $6,050. Meanwhile, Kenton's cast-iron version of the Woolworth Building sold for $6,600.

A cast-iron J. & E. Stevens Home Bank building commanded $16,500.

Big winners of the Bertoia auction included an 1885 Kyser & Rex Merry-Go-Round that sold for $30,800 and an 1882 Charles A. Bailey Springing Cat that brought $26,400.

Dolls

They're cute, lovable and find enough collectors to bring some great prices at auction. It seems no matter what the age of collectors, dolls are still a favorite.

Jumeaus were popular in the auction circuit this year, consistently fetching top prices.

A Richard W. Withington Inc. auction produced a sale of $9,200 for a bisque Depose Tete Jumeau doll that measured 19-1/2-inches and came with a bird cage, complete with a rocking bird.

In McMasters auction, a 19-inch Jumeau fashion doll sold for $2,025, while a 28-inch Tete Jumeau dressed in antique clothing with her original marked shoes realized $4,100.

Reaching an even higher price was a 28-inch Bebe Tete Jumeau in an antique ecru wool dress that hit $4,500 in an earlier McMasters auction. The auction also offered two S.F.B.J., the first being a laughing toddler that brought $1,700 and a Tete Jumeau with an S.F.B.J. face that captivated one lucky bidder for $2,200.

Schoenhut dolls were also prevalent, with many fetching four-figure

This 4-inch bisque Kewpie, complete with mandolin, brought $475 at a McMasters Auction. It was in Excellent condition.

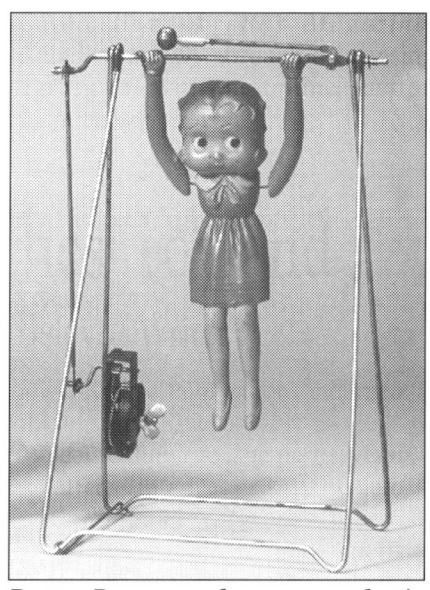

Betty Boop made an acrobatic appearance at a Skinner auction where she sold for $432. Made in Japan, the toy featured a clockwork motor.

Toy Shop Annual 2001

prices. Unique items at the McMasters auction included a Schoenhut doll house that realized $1,150, a carved hair boy for $1,300 and a 14-inch Rolly Doll that brought $800.

The same auction found new homes for an 11-1/2-inch Kestner 152 ($750) and a Simon & Halbig 1078 ($875).

The auction also featured a rare 4-inch Kewpie vase with a Doodle-dog, catching an astonishing bid of $2,600. Another Kewpie, complete with a mandolin, sold for $475.

Shirley Temple made a showing at McMasters, at least in doll form, through a 20-inch boxed Ideal version that realized $775.

Barbie

No fashion doll is more recognized than Barbie. Because of her longevity and popularity, she fares quite well at auction and is considered a perennial favorite.

A McMasters auction proved that vintage Barbie can, in fact, be affordable.

Besides the Ponytail #1 that sold for $8,700, other Barbies offered at the sale included a brunette Ponytail #5 in her box, complete with her accessories. It found a bid of $450.

Several boxed Bubblecut Barbies sold for $225, $375 and $155, respectively.

A Living Barbie with her box brought $205, while a Growing Pretty Hair Barbie realized $220.

Barbie wasn't the only star at the auction. Mattel's Twiggy doll, fashioned after the famous 1960s model, sold for $350.

Newer dolls included Barbie as Eliza Doolittle in *My Fair Lady*, NRFB (Never Removed From Box), $25; Midnight Waltz Barbie, NRFB, $15; Madison Avenue Barbie, NRFB, $105 and Soda Fountain Sweetheart Barbie, NRFB, $85.

Accessories for Barbie were also available at reasonable prices, including a Sorority Tea outfit for $30 in NRFB condition, a From Nine to Five Barbie accessory pack that went for $30 and a Hootenanny Barbie pack in NRFB condition that sold for $40.

Fetching the highest price among accessories at the McMasters auction was a Skater's Waltz Barbie accessory pack that sold for $215.

Establishing a record was one of Barbie's first outfits, selling for an incredible $6,000 at an online auction. The outfit, Gay Parisienne, was one of Barbie's three original 1959 outfits.

Tipp & Co. Mickey and Minnie Sells for $110,000

The tale of two Tipp & Co. Mickey and Minnie Motorcycle toys is like something out of *The Twilight Zone*.

If the toys were people, it would go something like this. Separated at birth, the Mickey and Minnie twins are reunited through a third party.

However, to be together again, a large amount of cash had to exchange hands.

Now for the real scenario.

Auctions in late 2000 by Randy Inman and Bill Bertoia both featured the rare Tipp & Co. Mickey and Minnie Motorcycle. The Inman sample included the only original box known to exist.

Billed as the top draw in the 1,000-lot Inman auction, it sold for $110,000, including the 10 percent buyer's premium.

In the Bertoia auction, the motorcycle, part of the esteemed collection of Pat and Doug Wengel, brought $52,800, including the 10 percent buyer's premium.

Here's where it gets weird. Both samples were purchased by the same New England couple. When asked why they purchased both items, their answer was simply, "Because it was there."

Another top seller in the Inman auction was a Mickey Mouse organ grinder wind-up tin litho with its original box.

Known as the Hurdy Gurdy, the item blew past its presale estimate and sold for $39,600.

Another Hurdy Gurdy in the Bertoia auction sold for $22,000.

The Tipp & Co. Mickey and Minnie Motorcycle sold for $110,000 in an Inman auction.

The Hurdy Gurdy starred in two auctions, bringing $39,600 at an Inman auction and $22,000 at a Bertoia auction.

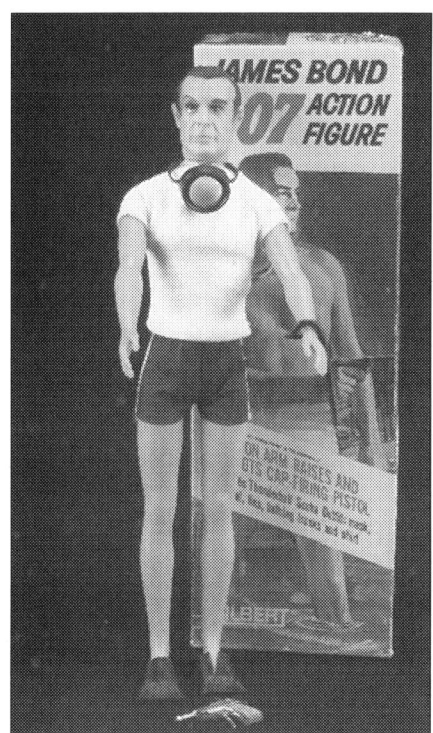

A Gilbert figure depicting Sean Connery as James Bond sold for $1,315.

G.I. Joe

Like Barbie is for girls, G.I. Joe is probably the most recognized icon for boys, commanding big prices for its vintage items.

Although only one year into the 21st century, the auction of the century could be the sale of the collection of recognized G.I. Joe creator Don Levine. Included in the sale were many prototype uniforms and figures.

The top price was for one of the most important G.I. Joe figures, an early prototype from Levine's personal collection. The handmade prototype found its second home through a bid of $18,600.

Other pieces that gathered astounding bids were an early Joe test shot head that brought $4,104 and an early printed Action Pilot box that garnered $8,971.

Another box that brought four figures was an Action Sailor box, selling for $3,749.

While boxes and cards for early G.I. Joes fared extremely well, the majority of the action figures did not find such high values, thanks to a recent slowdown in the market.

Included in this group was a Japanese Imperial Soldier which brought only $1,500. A Soldiers of the World German Stormtrooper prototype sold for $4,950.

At a McMasters auction, a G.I. Joe Action Marine in Very Good condition, complete with box, brought $105. McMasters also offered a Danger of the Depths set that had never been removed from its box. The gear, complete down to the SCUBA set and the shark, went for $160.

Action Figures

Action figures are living up to their name on the auction circuit, with fast and furious action being the norm.

As expected, vintage figures are attracting quite a bit of attention.

An Ideal Justice League of America Batman play set, made in 1967, sold for $10,221 at a Toy Scouts auction, despite being incomplete.

Other finds at the auction included an Aquaman-JLA play set box made by Multiple Toymakers in 1967 ($1,626) and a 1962 Lady Gaylord by Ideal ($943).

A Hake's auction turned up a Six Million Dollar Man Venus Space Probe that realized $900.

Christie's South Kensington held a TV Generation auction, turning up many familar action figures.

Nine Action Man figures were auctioned together, bringing in $1,785. The lot included Life Guard, Australian Jungle Fighter, German Stormtrooper and two cosutmes, among others.

As expected, James Bond did quite well in the TV Generation auction, with Gilbert action figures leading the way.

A James Bond figure, made in the likeness of the venerable Sean Connery, with original instructions and box, brought $1,315.

Odd Job, modeled in the likeness of Harold Sakata, with his original box outdid his nemesis, commanding $1,354.

Character Toys

Character toys were plentiful in

This Mickey Mouse Slate Dancer, made in Germany, sold for $22,000.

A collection of Action Man figures brought $1,785 at Christie's.

Toy Shop Annual 2001

auctions during 2000, and Mickey Mouse remained the perennial favorite.

Two fall auctions, Inman and Bertoia, had Mickey and friends as their main feature, displaying some amazing pieces. Along with the Tipp & Co. motorcycle and Hurdy Gurdy highlighted earlier, many rare pieces were also auctioned off.

Selling for $48,000 was a German-made Mickey Mouse with moving eyes and mouth dating back to the 1930s. One of the rarest of Mickey items, the legend on the back reads "By Exclusive Arrangement with Ideal Films Ltd. Registered No. 50841."

Another 1930s Mickey toy, a Spanish Nanny Minnie Mouse pushing Baby Felix in Pram, sold for $32,000. The figure was in Excellent condition.

The Bertoia auction also featured the most desirable of the three variations for the Mickey the Musical Mouse collectible. Made in Germany, this piece features Minnie pushing baby Mickey in a pram. The item, in Near Mint condition, brought $40,000.

A caged Felix? Retro clothing? No wonder a Minnie Mouse carrying Felix in cages brought $48,000. OK, it only depicted Felix in a cage, but its Pristine condition also helped boost the price.

Mickey stayed on a roll at the auction with $38,000 going to a Mickey Mouse "Pull on His Ear" money box, also in pristine condition.

This Mickey, with moving eyes and mouth, is one of the rarest Mickey items. It sold for $48,000.

Other top Mickey sales at the Bertoia auction included a Mickey Mouse and Felix sparkler ($20,000), a Mickey Mouse slate dancer ($22,000), a Mickey Mouse opening picnic basket holding Felix ($12,000) and a Mickey Mouse pram with its original box ($11,000).

In other character auctions, a 7-inch Fun-E-Flex Mickey Mouse figure by George Borgfeldt in a box in Good condition found a new buyer for $2,860 at an ITCA auction.

Adding character to a Lionel handcar, Mickey and Minnie were sold for $1,265 with a box in Very Good condition, although the legs on the figures had been repaired.

Hake's Americana & Collectibles featured a Mickey Mouse Bamby Bread sign for $736. The auction also found a buyer for a Seiberling Donald Duck figure after it reached $366.

Mickey and Minnie showed up at a later Hake's auction, where they proved their popularity is not waning. Proving that, A Minnie Mouse bisque figure sold for $1,065, putting her at the top of the auction sellers. A Mickey Mouse Boy Scout lamp failed to reach that amount, but still garnered $555.

Hake's also sold a Dick Tracy Crime Stoppers laboratory to a bidder for the healthy sum of $1,125.

An unusual Mickey Mouse popcorn popper was sold by Michael Auctions of Merrimack, N.H. The piece was so unique that it did not appear in any price guides. It featured a dome screen top, pan base and a 36-inch wooden handle. The final bid for this piece of Disneyana was $400,

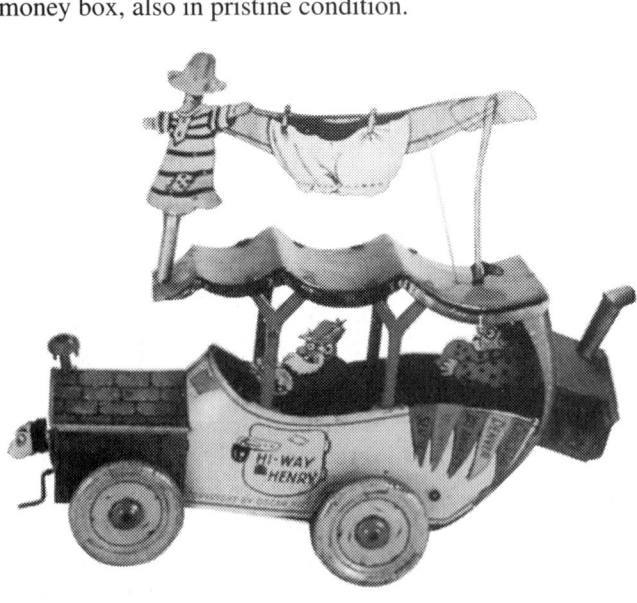

A unique Hi-Way Henry toy, circa 1925, sold for $3,205 during a Smith House Toys sale.

Looking for a Doll? Start Here!

While many nationwide auction houses conduct general auctions, several specialize in dolls of many eras. When looking for that perfect doll to begin or add to your collection, you might want to contact these specialty firms.

Theriault's
P.O. Box 151
Annapolis, MD 21404
(800) 638-9422

McMasters Doll Auctions
P.O. Box 1755
Cambridge, OH 43725
(800) 842-3526

Withington, Inc.
RD2 Box 440
Hillsboro, NJ 03244
(603) 464-3232

A Chein Popeye Bag Puncher slugged its way to a selling price of $7,700.

popcorn not included.

Bisque Disney figures were offered through Bertoia, with varying results. A Donald Duck figural toothbrush holder realized $990, while a Mickey Mouse and Pluto toothbrush holder garnered only $330.

Bullwinkle figures made a showing at a TV Toyland auction, and several figures found astounding prices. The top sale of the day went to an 8-inch Moonman figure from *The Bullwinkle Show,* reaching $2,013. A Sherman figure from *The Bullwinkle Show* also did well, finding a buyer for $699. The star of the show was not able to beat the Moonman, finding a sale price of $1,514.

While Mickey stole many of the headlines, Popeye had some success at auction as well.

Proving that you can't keep a good sailor down, tin items bearing Popeye's likeness commanded healthy prices at an ITCA auction earlier this year. The Chein Popeye with punching bag made a rare appearance at the auction where it sold for an auction-leading price of $5,445. Other Popeye items included a Linemar cyclist tin wind-up that found $1,540 and a Marx Bubble Blowing Popeye that realized $853.

Smith House Toys featured a variety of toys in a spring, 2000, auction, but two Popeye pieces stole the show. One of the rare items was a Popeye Olive Oyl Tank, one of only three known to exist.

Made in Japan, the 11-inch Linemar features Popeye pushing the tank forward and the tank them pushing him backwards. The item was in Excellent to Near Mint condition and sold for $9,000.

A Chein Popeye Bag Puncher, where Popeye swings at a celluloid punching bag, sold for $7,700.

At the same auction, a long-billed Donald Duck cyclist on a balloon tire tricycle brought $3,250.

A Hi-Way Henry collectible from the *Henry* comic strip sold for $3,205. The circa 1925 item showcases a bearded man with his fat wife in the back seat of a car. Her laundry dries on the clothesline attached to the roof.

Meanwhile, a 13-inch Marx Frankenstein that walks and bends over strolled away for $2,600.

Harkening back to the days of silent movies, a 1930s Schuco Charlie Chaplin doll, with its original box and key, sold for $1,220 at a Christie's auction.

Linemar's Popeye Olive Oyl Tank, one of only three known to exist, features Popeye pushing the tank, and it pushing back. It brought $9,000.

Nomura's Batman robot sailed to a sale of price of just over $1,500.

Toy Shop Annual 2001

TV Toys

The popularity of several toys at a TV Toyland auction demonstrated that some television shows endure long past the end of syndication.

A belt buckle advertising *Charlie's Angels* caught a high bid of $905, while a *Starsky and Hutch* racing set fetched $706.

One television show fan paid an out-of-this world price of $1,200 for a *Lost in Space* robot that communicated in Spanish. Aye Carumba!

Christie's South Kensington devoted an entire auction to TV Generation toys. One item that had collectors talking was a Batman robot by Nomura.

Made in the 1960s, the battery-operated robot, complete with his cape, sold for just over $1,500.

Batman-themed items did well at the auction, with a Corgi Gift Set, containing a Batmobile, Batboat with trailor and a 267 Batmobile in their original boxes, taking home nearly $1,700.

Another item that did well at the show was an A&M Bartram Dan Dare Space Ship Builder No. 3 in its original box. Unopened, the popular space toy brought $2,067.

A Corgi 227 Monkeemobile and a 805 Hardy Boys 1912 Rolls-Royce Silver Ghost, together, sold for $752.

Western Toys

Many collectors saddled up for some good old-fashioned Western toys this year, and they found many for the right price.

Western toys found serious buyers at an ITCA auction, perhaps aided by the wide selection of items present representing the history of Westerns on television.

The top price paid at the auction was $770 for a Gene Autry double-holster set with two guns that had been fired.

More affordable Autry memorabilia was also represented by a pair of chaps and a vest from 1950 that sold for $77.

A piece of Roy Rogers memorabilia was also available for bidding, with someone walking away with a pair of 1950s Roy Rogers chaps with studs and his initials for $138. At a separate auction, a boxed camera with Rogers' binoculars realized $476.

Lone Ranger toys found slightly higher prices and were well represented by a pair of never-worn Lone Ranger rubber boots that ran up to $303. A toothbrush holder from 1938 eventually brushed by the $200 mark to hit $231.

A Marx Best of the West Sam Cobra did not appear to be in as great demand, selling for only $66. The action figure came complete with 20 accessories and with a box in Excellent condition.

The auction also revealed a Hartland Ted Jeffords riding a horse, complete with an original box, for $149.

Chuck Hippler reported from ITCA that Annie Oakley items were commanding more attention from collectors recently, and the healthy prices from the auction helped

Auction Advice

Buying at auctions can be a fun, challenging and interesting way to acquire those treasured toys you desire. But if you're not familiar with how auctions are run, keep these tips in mind. Being informed will allow you to make smarter bids and get more satisfying results.

- **Examine the merchandise and ask questions**. Of course this isn't possible in phone, mail or online auctions, but it is possible to find out about an auctioneer's reputation. Ask others, was the "Mint" item actually in Mint condition? Ask a lot of questions about the item you'll be bidding on to avoid future regret or hassles.
- **Ask for photos** if they're available. If you're attending an auction, examine the condition of items and scout the competition. As you attend more auctions, you'll recognize some of the same faces and get a better handle on what particular people will be bidding on.
- **Register early**. To avoid tying up bidding lines, register early — even the night before if possible. For phone auctions, don't call at the final hour if you haven't already registered.
- **Bid wisely**. Don't open with an outrageously high bid — if you're the only bidder, you may end up paying too much. But also don't open with a laughably low bid either, you may not be taken seriously. Become familiar with presale estimates if they're offered.
- **Honor your bid**. If your bid wins, you've bought the piece — simple as that, right? It may sound elementary, but too often auctioneers are stiffed by bidders who don't pick up or pay for items. It's a sure way to ruin future relationships with auction houses.

The proof was in the packaging at a Skinner auction which featured original boxes for vintage Popeye toys. Many realized prices in the four-figure range.

Pictured are four of the robots included in a Skinner sale. From left to right are Daiyai's Space Conqueror Man of Tomorrow ($345), Daiya's Astronaut ($287.50), Cragstan's Astronaut ($747.50) and Cragstan's Great Astronaut ($1,092.50).

confirm his remarks.

A boxed Annie Oakley outfit found a new closet for $330, and a double holster with two guns in its original, colorful box saw a high bid of $358, making them among the highest prices paid for Western items at ITCA.

A Hopalong Cassidy gun-and-holster set sold at a TV Toyland auction for $1,380, one of the highest prices paid at auction for a toy from the show this year.

Toy Packages?!

Collectors rarely underestimate the value of a toy in its box, but at a recent Skinner auction, collectors valued the boxes alone.

Empty boxes that held presale estimates of $50 to $100 realized prices passing $2,500.

The top price paid for a box was $2,530, which bought a Popeye and Mean Man Fighters box by Linemar. The box was not only empty, but damaged!

Another piece of Popeye tin was absent from a Smoking Popeye box by Linemar, yet bidding still rose all of the way to $1,495. This example did contain an instruction sheet and an oil bottle for the toy.

A Popeye and Olive Oyl Stretchy Hand Car box sold for $1,265, while a Marx Popeye and Olive Oyl jiggers box was sent home with a new owner for $1,380. Other boxes included a damaged Chein Popeye Bag Puncher box that brought $1,092, and a Wimpy's Mechanical Tricycle box that realized $1,150.

Locomotives

All aboard the auction train. Locomotives are picking up steam with collectors.

A 1921 Bing spirit-fired 0-4-0 North-London-type Steam Tank Locomotive No. 1902, in immaculate shape, sold for $4,136 at a Christie's auction.

Others from the sale include a Bassett-Lowke electric BR Duchess of Montrose Locomotive No. 43262 and Tender from 1957 ($4,136), a Märklin clockwork MR 2-4-4 'Flat Iron' Tank Locomotive No. 2000 ($2,820) and a Bing for Bassett-Lowke spirit-fired 0-4-0 '112' Steam Locomotive ($3,195).

Robots

A Skinner auction featured metal men from the heyday of the tin figures. The auction leader was Mystery Action Mechanized Robot, also known as Robby Space Robot, when he sold for $6,900. The robot had flaws but included its box and packaging inserts. A reproduction of Robby showed up later, but it still fetched $805. The common and popular Cragstan Mr. Robot in white sold for $1,035, while Rosko's astronaut fetched $1,610.

Other robots from the Skinner auction included Cragstan's Radical Robot ($2,587), Taiya's Wheel-A-Gear Robot ($1,610) and Nomura's X-70 Tulip Head Robot ($1,849).

Other Notable Sales

Opfer's featured many interesting items from a private collector's collection including a pair of candy containers fashioned after early 20th-century football players by a German company. The figures, made of painted composition with cloth uniforms, loosely held a football in their left hands. The first figure sold for $6,270 while the other 19-inch figure sported a price of $4,950 due to a repaired hand and some paint loss.

A Zoltan the Fortune Teller amusement park machine went for $990, while a Strauss' tinplate Santee Claus, complete with a sleigh hauled by reindeer, brought $1,595.

Until Next Year

Each year brings new excitement to the toy hobby through auctions. Many rare pieces are unearthed and great prices are realized.

As online auctions grow and the established auction houses continue to bring in the top-dollar items, the future looks to bring in more of the same.

Atomic Robot Man, left, sold for $575, while Robot Lilliput by KT brought $3,450 at a Skinner auction.

Wave of the Future

Internet Provides Toys and Prices With a Simple Click

By Tom Bartsch

Computers used to only belong to such dignitaries as NASA to run the space shuttles. They weren't operated by 10-year-olds as a standard part of growing up.

Yet, that is what the world has come to. Wait, there's more.

Not only are computers commonplace, but on most there is a tool, a tool that allows users the chance to look at information without getting out of the chair.

It's called the Internet, and while schools laud it for its help in educating children, it's getting mixed reviews from those involved in the toy hobby.

On one hand, it brings out vintage pieces that would otherwise sit in dusty attics. On the other hand, the Internet provides the forum to bring out too much product, in essence flooding the market and bringing prices down.

Internet Auctions

How are all these attic finds getting in the marketplace?

Through Internet auctions. Anyone with a computer can be an instant buyer and seller of goods, regardless of his or her knowledge of the subject.

"Your Aunt Martha can put your cousin's long-forgotten Transformer on a scanner and run an auction that says 'Unknown Transformer, marked 1984' and get $100 all by herself," said John Marshall, author of five books on toys and character collectibles.

Jim Fay of Richard Johnson Toys in Prescott, Ariz., added "There [are] a lot of people that sell older pieces over the Internet. But there [are] a lot of people that are on there that don't quite know what they're doing.

"They list something new that doesn't fetch a great price, and they list it 20 times in a row."

Robert Johnson feels inexperi-

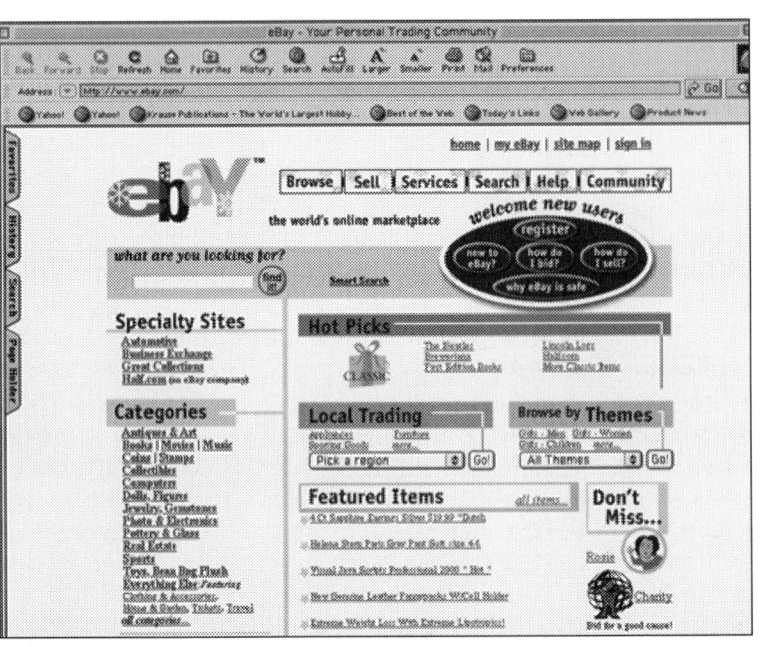

Online auctions, such as eBay, the leader in the field, have brought much more product and customers into the toy market.

enced Internet sellers needs to get all their facts right to compete with knowledgeable dealers.

"I have often seen toys advertised as complete when they are, in fact, missing parts," Johnson said of online auction descriptions. "This makes those amateurs' condition ratings unreliable at best and downright ignorant at worst.

"And as the collector is being bombarded with 'All Sales Final,' then it just comes down to caveat emptor — buyer beware."

From the online giant of eBay, to others such as Yahoo!, Amazon and SoldUSA.com, not to mention the smaller online dealers, toy enthusiasts have their pick of where to go in purchasing or selling their favorite toys.

However, with so much product out there, what was once a matter of scanning the toy shelves for the object of your desire, now consists of endless scrolling through Internet "pages" in hopes the G.I. Nurse listed is the original Hasbro figure from 1967 and not some B-rated movie.

Fay said about wading through the listings, "It kind of makes it hard to sift through the items when you have five million newer things going on that you're not interested in. There are some dedicated people out there that really search for certain things and know what they're looking for."

Price Wars

Before the impact of online auctions, auction prices realized often dictated the market price for toys. If a rare tin wind-up sold for $1,500, another one of the same condition was marked for that on another dealer's shelf.

But now with the Internet bringing all these new products into the marketplace, the impact on prices hasn't been favorable. In many cases, prices have diminished.

Johnson said while more people are "plugged in," it isn't helping the high-end pieces.

"From a pricing standpoint, prices

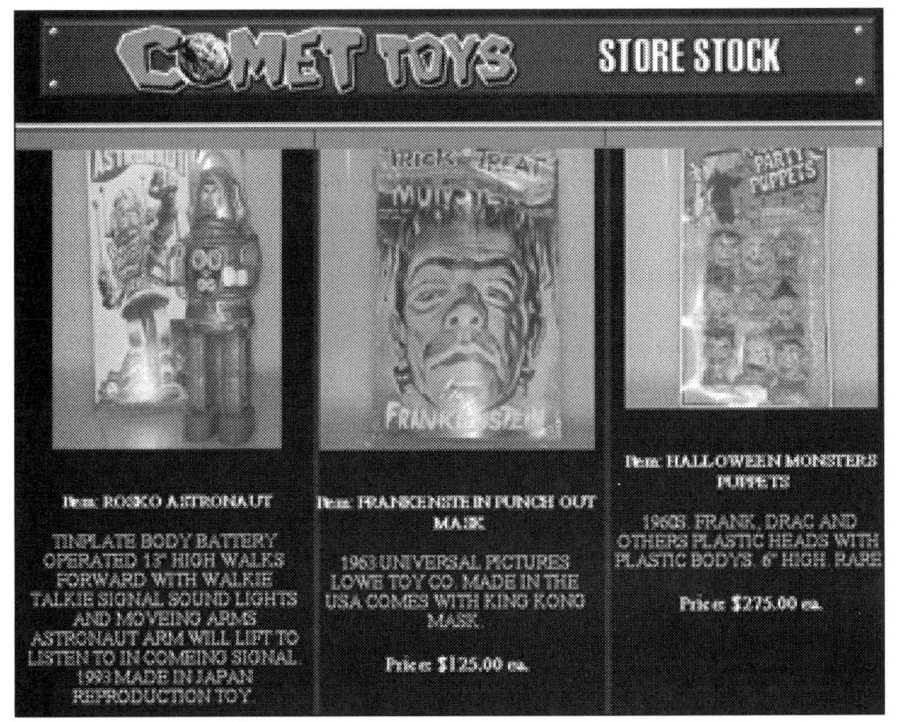

Robert Johnson's site, www.comettoys.com, has helped him generate more sales and he doesn't feel that will dissipate. "We are living in the future," he said.

have fallen on the most expensive toys but have risen for most mid-price toys ($500 to $1,200)," he said.

Fay compares the Internet toy market to a lake. There's only so much water that can be drained before it's empty.

"Right now, it seems there [are] so many pieces on eBay for sale [but] there's only a certain amount of money there to buy pieces over the Internet," he said. "It kind of depends on what you're selling on there. Some of the newer stuff doesn't necessarily go for that much on there compared to shop prices.

"If it's an older, fairly hard-to-find piece, they seem to fetch pretty good prices over the Internet."

Marshall agrees that the hard-to-find items in good condition do quite well on the Internet.

"Prices on rare, Mint-in-Package items are through the roof," Marshall said. "Recently, a relatively obscure monster figure from the 1970s, the Yeti from the Famous Monsters line, went for over $700 on eBay.

"If you had asked me a week earlier, I would have stated its top price was $300 to $400. It's not even one of the good [figures] in the line."

On the Flip Side

As any one in sales knows, prices are one thing, but without customers, prices mean little.

This is where dealers find themselves. Hop on the Internet bandwagon and have prices fluctuate or decrease. Ignoring the Internet, however, may see many possible sales get bypassed.

As expected, many dealers have opted to do a little of both. Many have kept their storefronts open while offering the same goods on their Web sites.

Having a Web site also allows customers to view pieces on the screen and get prices, rather than sending for a catalog. It saves time and money for both sides. Contact information like phone numbers and e-mail addresses on the Web site has sped up the rate of communication as well.

Then there is the matter of toy shows. Why do collectors need to go to these when all they have to do is flip a switch on the computer? It's no secret that attendance is declining at toy shows across the country.

"Toy shows are dying out because it is easier to sell obscure items, very small items and very large items over the Internet as opposed to dragging them to shows and risking loss, damage and apathy on part of the patrons," Marshall said.

However, all is not lost. Dealers and collectors still flock to toy shows to see the products in person and to meet with those in the hobby.

What's Ahead?

So, the toy market has gone from being a face-to-face operation to one of cyberspace. As we venture further into the next millennium, this trend doesn't look like it's going to disappear.

Prices will continue to drop in some areas, but soon it will be standard in the hobby and the controversy will dissipate. Until then, we boldly move forward.

In a practice not seen many years ago, Richard Johnson Toys sells its products online, providing customer prices and contact information.

Toy Shop Annual 2001

SHOWCASE EXPRESS
EXPANDABLE DISPLAY SYSTEM...
GROWS WITH YOUR COLLECTION

64th scale with Monza track

43RD SCALE with Monza track

25th scale with Monza track

64th scale with Step shelf

- Expandable Display System
- Join top to bottom or end to end
- Monza track or Step shelf available
- Photo background or mirrors optional
- Anodized aluminum with dust proof window
- The most versatile collectors display system available
- Dealer inquires welcome

For more information concerning our Modular Display system, call 714-842-5564 X: 29. or www.showcase-express.com

---

5500 up-to-date values • 500 full-color photographs

Toy Shop's ACTION FIGURE PRICE GUIDE

EDITED BY ELIZABETH A. STEPHAN

STAY ON TOP OF THE ACTION

Toy Shop's Action Figure Price Guide
edited by Elizabeth A. Stephan

Does your Luke Skywalker action figure have a telescoping light saber? Have you ever wondered if it has any value? You might be surprised by the value of ol' Luke had you not played with him. What about those Transformer figures that were all the rage 15 years ago? Toy Shop's Action Figure Price Guide will help answer all of your action figure questions. From the publishers of Toy Shop, this up-to-date guide will prove to be indispensable with over 2500 listings, 5,000 values and 500 photos, not to mention the in-depth history and market update of the action figure hobby.

Softcover • 8-1/4 x 10-7/8 • 256 pages
500 color photos
Item# ACFIG • $24.95

NEW

To place a credit card order or for a FREE all-product catalog, call

800-258-0929 Offer TGHT

M-F, 7 am - 8 pm • Sat, 8 am - 2 pm, CST
Krause Publications, Offer TGHT, P.O. Box 5009, Iola, WI 54945-5009
www.krausebooks.com

Shipping and Handling: $3.25 1st book; $2 ea. add'l. Foreign orders $20.95 1st item, $5.95 each add'l.
Sales tax: CA, IA, IL, PA, TN, VA, WA, WI residents please add appropriate sales tax.
Satisfaction Guarantee: If for any reason you are not completely satisfied with your purchase, simply return it within 14 days and receive a full refund, less shipping.

Retailers call toll-free 888-457-2873 ext 880, M-F, 8 am - 5 pm

Buying and Selling
Robots, Space Toys & Superheroes
Top Prices Paid

See our new updated web site: www.bergintoys.com

MARK BERGIN
Hundreds of Toys for Sale
mbergin@top.monad.net
Tel: (603) 924-2079   Fax: (603) 924-2022

P.O. Box 631163
Houston, TX 77263-1163
Phone/Fax: 1-713-785-1566
Email: scifitoyz@msn.com
SI-FI TOYS, MODELS, AND MORE...
Payment: Checks, M/O'S, or Paypal. TX residents must add an 8 1/4% sales tax.
Visit our Web site: http://www.scifitoyz.com
We Carry All Polar Lights Models, J Lightning, Sci Fi Movie and TV related toys, Batman
We are a Diamonds Distributor
ALWAYS CALL OR E-MAIL FOR AVAILABILITY!

CRM2000

PL5002 Addams family haunted house/glow in dk	$15.69
PL5004 Mummy's chariot	11.69
PL5005 Bride of Frankenstein	17.69
PL5006 Frankenstein flevver	13.69
PL5012 Mummy's chariot dragster(lmtd)/glow in dk	11.69
PL5013 Munsters living room	19.69
PL5014 Caspers undertaker dragster (lmtd)	19.68
PL5015 Wolfmans rod wagon	13.69
PL5016 King Kong's thronester hot rod	15.69
PL5017 The Green Hornet black beauty car	16.09
PL5018 The Wolfman (Lon Chaney Jr.)	17.69
PL5019 Lost in space robot and Dr. Smith	19.69
PL5020 Customizing monster kit #1	12.99
PL5021 Customizing monster kit #2	12.99
PL5022 Sleepy Hollow	17.50
PL5023 Mummy w/coffin 1999 version	19.99
PL5025 Robby the robot- Forbidden Planet	15.50
PL5026 Dracula's Dragster	17.69
PL5027 Phantom of the Opera with organ	21.29
PL5028 Bates Psycho house /Hitchcock classic	17.69
PL5029 Crash Bandacoot	14.32
PL5029 Go-Carts	18.98
PL5030 Lost in Space robot 7"	15.69
PL5031 Lost in Space Cyclops	14.69
PL5032 Lost in Space Cyclops with chariot	19.69
PL5033 Lost in Space Jupiter II	19.69
PL5035 James Bond as 007/ with pistol	15.69
PL5036 Odd Job from 007/ Goldfinger	15.69
PL5061 3 Stooges/ Larry with torch	18.98
PL5062 3 Stooges/ Moe with vase	18.98
PL5063 3 Stooges/ Curley with torch	18.98
PL5090 The Huntchback	18.98
PL5091 LaGuillotine	16.50
PL5092 Salem Witch	16.98
PL5093 Dick Tracy	15.50
PL6700 Speed Racer Mach 5	16.50
PL7052 Godzilla	16.50
PL7053 Rodan	16.50
PL7501 Creature from the Black Lagoon	21.95
PL7075 Godzilla	17.69
78008 James Bond Cars	48.99
78898 Speed Racer 2000	19.50
78901 Speed Racer 2000 Special Edition	19.50
78892 True Grit 1st Release	21.95
78892B True Grit 2nd Release	23.99
78888 .Com Racers	19.50
363-05 Speed Racer First Shots	41.99
78889 Y2K Bugs- Target Exclusives	19.50
78886 Frightning Lightning 2	19.50
78891 First Shots	41.99
78890 Wacky Racers	16.00
784954 Lost in Space	19.99
78990 Team Lightning 1	14.99
79999 Team Lightning 2	19.99
79998 Monopoly Cars	38.95

THE Joe DEPOT, INC.
Authentic — G.I. Joe World Headquarters — Equipment

WORLD'S LARGEST SELECTION OF G.I. JOE FIGURES & ACCESSORIES

Phone or FAX (215) 721-9749
P.O. Box 228, Kulpsville, PA 19443-0228
E-mail: GIJOE@FAST.NET

http:/www.ewtech.com/gijoe/

ALWAYS BUYING G.I. JOE COLLECTIONS

Hot Wheels • Match Box • CORGI
MARX • Captain Action • Major Matt Mason
• Tin Toys • Steel Toys.
And other toys from the 1950's thru 1980's.

We Pay Highest Prices for Toy Collections of Any Size. No collection too small or too large.

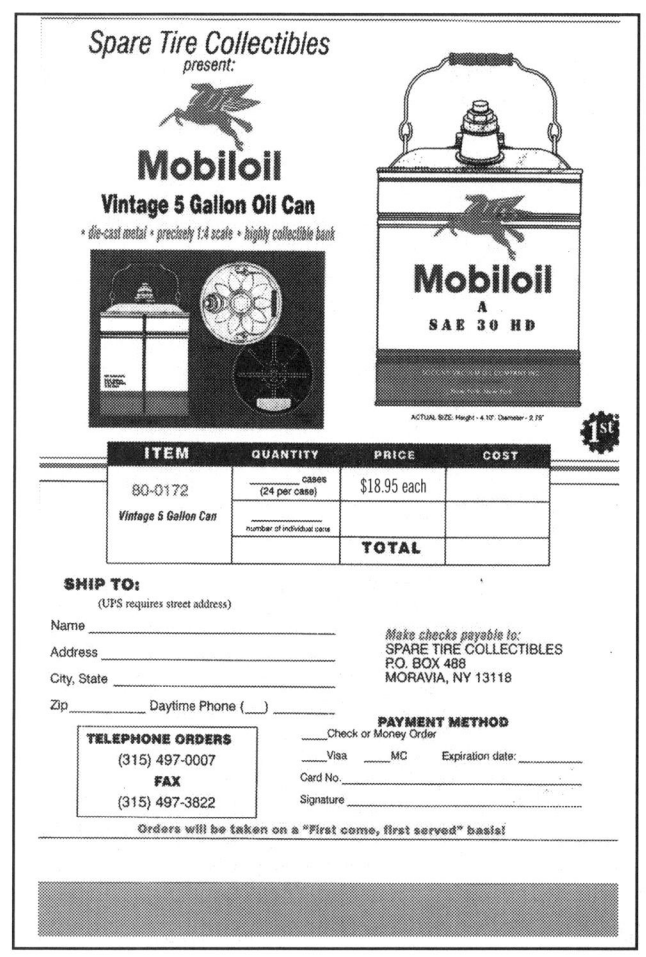

Spare Tire Collectibles present:

Mobiloil
Vintage 5 Gallon Oil Can
* die-cast metal * precisely 1:4 scale * highly collectible bank

ACTUAL SIZE: Height - 4.13", Diameter - 2.75"

ITEM	QUANTITY	PRICE	COST
80-0172 Vintage 5 Gallon Can	cases (24 per case) / number of individual cans	$18.95 each	
		TOTAL	

SHIP TO:
(UPS requires street address)
Name _____
Address _____
City, State _____
Zip _____ Daytime Phone (___)

Make checks payable to:
SPARE TIRE COLLECTIBLES
P.O. BOX 488
MORAVIA, NY 13118

TELEPHONE ORDERS
(315) 497-0007
FAX
(315) 497-3822

PAYMENT METHOD
___ Check or Money Order
___ Visa ___ MC Expiration date: _____
Card No. _____
Signature _____

Orders will be taken on a "First come, first served" basis!

More Great Books For Serious Collectors

O'Brien's Collecting Toy Cars & Trucks
Identification & Value Guide, 3rd Edition
edited by Elizabeth A. Stephan
This indispensable identification and price guide for toy cars and trucks is now more comprehensive and easier to use than ever, featuring a new alphabetical organization, a more in-depth table of contents, expanded categories and many new photos for easier identification. You are sure to find the car/truck you need within over 300 categories and more than 15,000 listings; some of which are listed no where else. Listings are usually priced in three grades of condition for a largest-ever total of nearly 45,000 current market value prices.
Softcover • 8-1/2 x 11 • 640 pages
2,500 b&w photos
16-page color section
Item# TCT3 • $27.95

Ultimate Price Guide to Fast Food Collectibles
edited by Elizabeth A. Stephan
Ultimate Guide to Fast Food Collectibles features premiums from Arby's to White Castle and provides readers with the most up-to-date pricing. With over 1800 values and 500 photographs, this book is sure to become a standard in the hobby.
Softcover • 8-1/2 x 11
272 pages
500 b&w photos
16-page color section
Item# FASFD • $24.95

Stock Car Model Kit Encyclopedia and Price Guide
by Bill Coulter
This book lists and values more than 800 stock car models (nearly every one ever produced) and pictures over 300 models, from 1:43 to 1:24 scale and larger. It also contains valuable insights and tips for modelers and collectors.
Softcover • 8-1/2 x 11 • 208 pages
400 b&w photos • 40 color photos
Item# STMK • $19.95

100 Greatest Baby Boomer Toys
by Mark Rich
Relive your childhood with this nostalgic picture book of toys from your past. You'll reminisce as you look at the photos and read about the history of these toys, whether you're a baby boomer, a collector or just looking for a fabulous gift. The 100 greatest toys are ranked in popularity and value listings are included for many more. And, if you're not already a collector, you may become one after seeing the values of some of those deep-in-the-closet keepsakes.
Softcover • 8-1/4 x 10-7/8
208 pages • 250 color photos
Item# BOOM • $24.95

O'Brien's Collecting Toys
9th Edition
edited by Elizabeth Stephan
This is the best encyclopedic, photo-intensive price guide and reference book for more than 16,000 vintage and obscure toys from the late 1880s to today. All of the 45,000 prices have been reviewed and updated from the eighth edition, with many increasing.
Softcover • 8-1/2 x 11
768 pages
3,500 b&w photos
6-page color section
Item# CTY09 • $28.95

Vintage Toys
Robots and Space Toys
by Jim Bunte, Dave Hallman, and Heinz Mueller
Packed with beautiful, large color photographs and encyclopedic-style details, this volume focuses on tin toys manufactured from World War I through the 1970s. American, British, French, German and Spanish robots and space toys are featured, but special coverage is given to Japanese tin toys. More than 300 different items are illustrated and profiled, along with up-to-date collector values.
Softcover • 8-1/2 x 11 • 192 pages
400 color photos
Item# AT1025 • $26.95

To place a credit card order or for a FREE all-product catalog call
800-258-0929 Offer TYBR
M-F, 7 am - 8 pm • Sat, 8 am - 2 pm, CST
Krause Publications, Offer TYBR, P.O. Box 5009, Iola, WI 54945-5009
www.krausebooks.com

Toy Shop

2001 Toys & Prices
8th Edition
edited by Sharon Korbeck and Elizabeth A. Stephan
One of today's hottest collecting areas - TV Toys - now has its own chapter, highlighting your favorites from the 1940s through the 1990s. Space toys fans will now have an easier-to-use section, including a spotlight on ultra-hot robots. Both the casual collector and veteran enthusiast will find over 58,000 values on more than 20,000 toys including cast-iron banks, lunch boxes, board games, Barbie, PEZ, space toys, Fisher-Price, Hot Wheels, restaurant toys and more.
Softcover • 6 x 9 • 936 pages
700 b&w photos • 8-page color section
Item# TE08 • $18.95

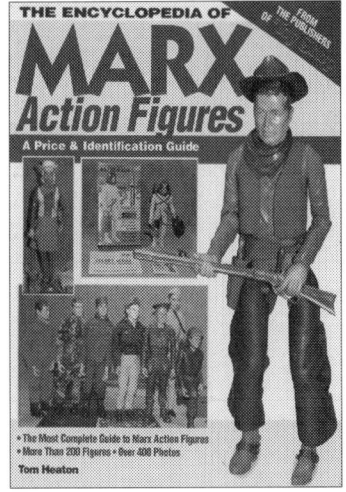

The Encyclopedia of Marx Action Figures
A Price & Identification Guide
by Tom Heaton
This book is a complete guide to the over 230 Marx action figures produced, with detailed photos that show the boxes and accessories, allowing you to identify and value your figures. Values are given in three grades: mint in box/carded; poor box and most accessories; loose with some accessories.
Softcover • 8-1/2 x 11
192 pages
425 color photos
Item# MARX • $24.95

Marx Toys Sampler
Playthings from an Ohio Valley Legend
by Michelle Smith
If "Marx mania" has you in its grasp, here's a new book that's sure to capture your attention and interest. In this first behind-the-scenes look at the internal operations and production output of the Marx Toys plant in Glen Dale, West Virginia, you'll learn about Marx toys and the people who produced them. And, you'll find a comprehensive listing, supported by more than 150 photographs, representing over thirty years of lithographed metal and cast plastic toy production-a valuable tool for identifying and dating items in your own collection of Marx Playsets, doll houses, figures, and other toys.
Softcover • 8-1/2 x 11 • 192 pages
150 b&w photos • 32-page color section, 100 color photos
Item# MXTS • $26.95

Saturday Morning TV Collectibles
'60s '70s '80s
by Dana Cain
Zoinks! Do you remember all of the Saturday morning kids' programs? This encyclopedia of 1960s to 1980s kids' show collectibles will certainly refresh your memory. If you're already a veteran collector, this guide is great, as it features in-depth listings, prices and photos of your favorite Saturday morning program collectibles. If you're a novice or beginning hobbyist, you'll find your favorite character collectibles and how much you should pay. More than 3,500 items priced.
Softcover • 8-1/2 x 11 • 288 pages
750 b&w photos • 16-page color section, 200 color photos
Item# TOON • $24.95

Toy Shop's Action Figure Price Guide
edited by Elizabeth A. Stephan
Does your Luke Skywalker action figure have a telescoping light saber? Have you ever wondered if it has any value? You might be surprised by the value of ol' Luke had you not played with him. What about those Transformer figures that were all the rage 15 years ago? Toy Shop's Action Figure Price Guide will help answer all of your action figure questions. This up-to-date guide will prove to be indispensable with over 2500 listings, 5000 values and 500 photos, not to mention the in-depth history and market update of the action figure hobby.
Softcover • 8-1/4 x 10-7/8 • 256 pages • 500 color photos
Item# ACFIG • $24.95

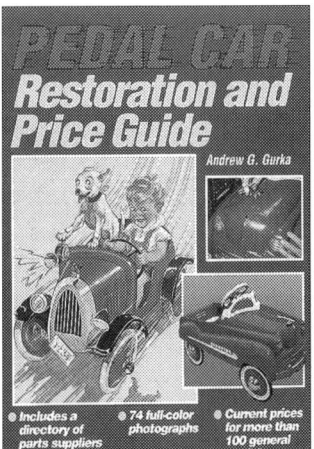

Pedal Car Restoration and Price Guide
by Andrew G. Gurka
Now, learn how to restore pedal cars, find parts and date cars by comparison to automotive styling trends. Price guide uncovers the latest values.
Softcover • 8-1/2 x 11
240 pages
316 b&w photos
16-page color section
Item# PCR01 • $24.95

Shipping and Handling: $3.25 1st book; $2 ea. add'l. Foreign orders $20.95 1st item, $5.95 ea. add'l.
Sales tax: CA, IA, IL, PA, TN, VA, WA, WI residents please add appropriate sales tax.

Satisfaction Guarantee: If for any reason you are not completely satisfied with your purchase, simply return it within 14 days and receive a full refund, less shipping.
Retailers call toll-free 888-457-2873 ext 880, M-F, 8 am - 5 pm

Toy Shop Annual 2001

SAVE $5.00
NOW
TOY CARS & MODELS

Expanded Issues
All 4 Color
Bold New Design

FUELED BY PREMIUM EDITORIAL COVERAGE INCLUDING:

- Hot Wheels • Matchbox
- Revell-Monogram
- Brooklin • Minichamps
- Racing Champions/Ertl

Subscribe Today!
1 yr (12 issues) only $19.98

To place a credit card order or for a FREE all-product catalog Call

800-258-0929 Offer ABAX18

M-F, 7 am - 8 pm • Sat, 8 am - 2 pm, CST

Mail orders on a 3x5 card to: **Toy Shop, Offer ABAX18** • 700 E. State St., Iola, WI 54990-0001
www.toycarsmag.com

Toy Dealer Directory

Action Figures

All Star Celebrity Collect
5637 Keokuk Ave.
Woodland Hills, CA 91367
818-884-2969

Bruce Hemmah
100 Main St. W
Cannon Falls, MN 55009
507-263-4704

Deep End Collectibles
P.O. Box 556
Mansfield Center, CT 06250
860-450-1173

Figures
P.O. Box 19482
Johnston, RI 02919
401-946-5720

Josh Vilensky
34 S Washington Ave.
Bergenfield, NJ 07621
914-354-0594

Just Be Distribution
111 NW 2nd Ave.
Portland, OR 97209
503-796-2733

New Force Comics & Collectibles
5834 SW 146th Ct.
Miami, FL 33183
850-769-1745

Old Forest Press
223 Wall St.
Huntington, NY 11743
516-423-1801

Rebel Toy
2300 California St.
Placentia, CA 92870
714-579-0673

Star Show Collectibles
6079 40th Ave.
Alta, IA 51002
515-321-0489

Village Comics
214 Sullivan St.
New York, NY 10012
212-777-2770

Entertainment Earth
12730 Raymer St., Ste. 1
North Hollywood, CA 91605
818-255-0090

Advertising Toys

Concord Confections
345 Courtland Ave.
Courtland, ON L4K5A6
905-660-8989

Airplanes

Quality Steins & Collectibles
886 W. Wooster St.
Bowling Green, OH 43402
419-353-6847

Wings and Wheels
66 Whittier Rd.
Medford, MA 02155

Antique Toys

Darrow's Fun Antiques
1101 First Ave.
New York, NY 10021
212-838-0730

Auctions

Hake's Americana & Collectibles
P.O. Box 1444
York, PA 17405
717-848-1333

John Bell Auctions
1112 W. 15th St.
Chandler, OK 74834
405-258-1511

Randy Inman Auctions
P.O. Box 726
Waterville, ME 04903
207-872-6900

Auctionworks.Com
1776 Peachtree St. NW, Ste. 600
N.
Atlanta, GA 30309
877-668-2655

Banks

Toy Box Collectibles
Specializing in Canadian Toys
We also Carry Dinky, Corgi Parts
Also Other Diecast Toys and Sci-Fi, etc.
SELL ★★★ BUY ★★★ TRADE
525 Highland Rd. W   Phone (519) 570-3120
Suite #304   Fax (519) 744-7621
Kitchener ON N2M SP4   E-mail toybox@bond.net
Canada
CANADA

Books

Blystone's
2132 Delaware Ave.
Pittsburgh, PA 15218
412-371-3511

Windmill Press
P.O. Box 56551
Sherman Oaks, CA 91413
818-704-6650

Character Toys

Decades
110 W. 4th St.
Royal Oak, MI 48067
248-546-9289

STAR WARS
Vintage carded figures
POTF NIKTO $1250
POTF AT-AT DRIVER $650
Loose cardboard Death Star $350
f/p 01161297705163
e-mail: Mangil@hotmail.com

The world's first antique toy shop
Chick Darrows
FUN ANTIQUES
Featuring collectibles
of every Persrxription
vintage toys, dolls, radios, banks, Trek™, autographs,
toy soldiers, games, animation art, memorabilia
Buy - Sell - Trade - Rentals
1101 First Ave. btwn 60th + 61st Sts.
New York, NY 10021
Ph: 212-838-0730
Fax: 212-838-3617
hours Tues-Friday 12pm-7pm
Sat 12-5pm
Sunday and custom visits by appt.
www.fun-antiques.com
Catering to the seekers of the unusual since 1962

Toy Shop Annual 2001

John's Collectible Toys
57 Bay View Dr.
Shrewsbury, MA 01545
508-797-0023

M & J Variety
932 East Blvd.
Alpha, NJ 08865
908-213-9099

Clubs

The M&Ms Collectors Club
"Collecting Everything Ever Made"
Jinni Wolfe - President
P.O. Box 153
Lake Harmony, PA 18624
570-722-1020
www.mnmclub.com
Annual Dues: $20
Bi-Monthly Newsletter Annual Convention

Die-Cast Banks

Homestead Collectibles
P.O. Box 173
Mill Hall, PA 17751
570-726-3597

Die-Cast Cars

Diecast Toys
P.O Box 30
Manhattan, IL 60442
815-478-4202

Dave's Diecast
207 Kennedy Dr.
Bangor, PA 18013
610-588-9984

Smith Model Import
18413 Rt. 700
Hiram, OH 44234
440-834-8817

MTR Enterprises
P.O. Box 617
Stevensville, MI 49127
906-296-0804

Performance Miniatures
www.performanceminiatures.com
Call for Free Catalog
1-800-931-1227
DIE CAST MODELS

Dolls

Doll & Hobby Shoppe
138 S. Woodland Blvd.
Deland, FL 32720
904-734-3200

Raggedys and Teddys Company
1850 Gingercake Cr. #103
Rock Hill, SC 29732
803-980-8489

The Raggedy's & Teddy's Co.
Buying/Selling old Raggedy Ann doll
& Teddy Bear collections.
Contact:
Larry Vaughan
1850 Gingercake Cr. #103, Rock Hill, SC 29732-7446
809-980-8489
raggedyman@aol.com   www.raggedyann.cc

Figures

Best Comics
25202 Northern Blvd.
Little Neck, NY 11362
718-279-2099

G.I. Joe

Cotswold Collectibles
P.O. Box 716
Freeland, WA 98249
360-331-5331

Joe Depot
P.O. Box 228
Kulpsville, PA 19443
215-721-9749

Club Hair For G.I. Joe
P.O. Box 2141
Yakima, WA 98907
509-965-5920

Old Joe Infirmary
353 E. 10th St., Ste. E
Gilroy, CA 95020
408-847-4897

Hot Wheels

Adkins Collectible Toys
9725 S. 54th St.
Franklin, WI 53132
414-761-1020

Die-Cast Warehouse
24 Pearl St.
Biddeford, ME 04005
413-473-6101

Lunch Boxes

Frantic City Toys
4232 Danor Dr.
Reading, PA 19605
610-929-8859

Miscellaneous Toys

Allan Kevorkian
204 Rounds Ave.
Providence, RI 2907
401-781-6264

Billy Galaxy
912 W. Burnside St.
Portland, OR 97209
503-227-8253

Cool Stuff Video
P.O. Box 1544
Elk Grove, CA 95759
916-686-0645

Crazyladycollectibles
28 Edgemoor Rd.
Timonium, MD 21093
410-252-0379

Creepy
3770 Vinton Ave., Apt 3
Los Angeles, CA 90034
310-842-4820

Ghoulie Motors
674 Portland St.
Rochester, NH 03867
603-335-0555

Heroes Unlimited
P.O. Box 453
Oradell, NJ 07649
201-261-4982

Home Craft Software
20676 SW Elk Horn Ct.
Tualatin, OR 97062
503-692-3732

Klaatu's Out-Of-This-World
820 Caron Circle NW
Atlanta, GA 30318
404-792-2929

Mrs. Miller's Memorabilia
70 Greenwich Ave., # A
New York, NY 10011
718-225-0572

View-Masters
Alan Goldberg
Sawyers GAF
E-mail address: algold4452@aol.com
461-2 Willow Rd. East
Staten Island, NY 10314
718-761-0864
Want Lists Solicited

Norman's Olde Store
126 W. Main St.
Washington, NC 27889
252-946-3448

Old Tyme Toystore
3914a N. Davis Hwy.
Pensacola, FL 32503
850-429-0333

Shadowland
31 E. Centre St.
Mahanoy City, PA 17948
610-437-0189

Stephen M Russo
P.O. Box 150
Revere, MA 02151
617-389-7325

Tom Snook
478 Sandy Way
Benicia, CA 94510
510-787-3283

Toys Toys Toys
4144 Amboy Rd.
Staten Island, NY 10308
718-980-3939

Good Stuff To Go
12405 Reeds St.
Shawnee Mission, KS 66209
913-451-9233

Great Jones World
P.O. Box 779
New Hope, PA 18938
215-862-5411

Movie / TV Show Toys
D.C. Hollis
P.O. Box 65
Mount Tabor, NJ 07878
973-398-1796

Specializing in
THE SIMPSONS merchandise
P.O. Box 981,
Monterey Park, CA 91754
http://www.simpsational.com
E-Mail: simpsational@earthlink.com
Phone: 323-415-6446

Monsters In Motion
330 E. Orangethorpe Ave.
Placentia, CA 92870
714-577-8863

Simpson's Express
P.O. Box 981
Monterey Park, CA 91754
323-415-6446

Steve's Lost Land of Toys
3572 Turner Ct.
Fremont, CA 94536
510-795-0598

Truly Unique Collectibles
301 Rte 17 S, #9
Hillburn, NY 10931
914-357-7411

Play Sets
Amok Time Toys
2941 Hempstead Turnpike
Levittown, NY 11756
516-520-0975

Great Old Toys
36 Macarthur Blvd.
Danvers, MA 01923
978-774-3955

Plush
Collectible Exchange
1527 Bourbon Parkway
Streamwood, IL 60107
630-736-6237

Robots
Art 'N' Things
133 Anderson Ave.
Fairview, NJ 07022
201-943-2288

Ray Rohr
P.O. Box 711
Kirkland, WA 98083
425-823-9530

Richard Johnson
P.O. Box 27093
Prescott Valley, AZ 86312
520-775-4714

Mark Bergin
2 E. Mountain Rd.
Peterborough, NH 03458
603-924-2079

Services
Collectibles Insurance Agency
P.O. Box 1200
Westminster, MD 21158
410-873-8833

Dave Cohen & Associates
640 Ackerman Ave.
Westwood, NJ 07675
201-666-2222

Showcase Express
714-842-5564

Shows
Bruce Beimers
1720 Rupert St. NE
Grand Rapids, MI 49525
616-361-9887

Old Mother's Cupboard
150 N. Wood Duck Ave.
Sanger, CA 93657
888-558-8697

Southeastern Collectible
1819 Peeler Rd.
Vale, NC 28168
704-276-1670

Motoring in Miniature
25 Tiernon Park
Buffalo, NY 14223
716-837-4023

My Mummy Productions
936 South St.
Wrentham, MA 02093
508-384-8491

Atlantic Group
P.O. Box 217
Swansea, MA 02777
508-379-9733

Antique World Shows
29718 N. Virginia Ln.
Wauconda, IL 60084
847-526-1645

Space Toys
Brian Semling
W730 State Road 35
Fountain City, WI 54629
608-687-9572

Cloud City
4151 Berkford Cir NE
Atlanta, GA 30319
678-405-7868

CRM2000
P.O. Box 631163
Houston, TX 77263-1163

Earth,The
4166 Allendale Dr., Apt 3
Cincinnati, OH 45209
513-731-8697

Tally Ho Studio
639 Park Ave. SW
Canton, OH 44706
330-452-4488

Time & Space Toys
8313 Graceway Dr.
Lorton, VA 22079
730-339-8576

Trading Cards
Barrington Square
P.O. Box 310
West Dundee, IL 60118
847-426-2020

Trucks
Ronald Burmester
631-758-3455

Hamilton-Wilber
P.O. Box 488
Moravia, NY 13118
315-497-0007

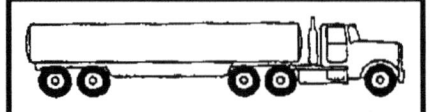

HESS • TEXACO
As well as other oil company promotional trucks & related items
Buy • Sell • Trade
Ron Burmester
(631) 758-3455
Fax (631) 758-3979

Vehicle Toys
Bruce Johnson Toy Talk
702 Steeplechase Rd.
Landisville, PA 17538
717-898-2932

Budget-Minder Collectible
701 E Bay St.
Charleston, SC 29403
843-577-7695

California Collectables
1060 E. 11th St.
Oakland, CA 94606
510-653-1310

Evers Toy Store
204 1st Ave. E
Dyersville, IA 52040
319-875-2438

Full Grid
3537 Torrance Blvd., Ste 25
Torrance, CA 90503
310-792-0308

Granite State Collectables
103 Main St.
New Ipswich, NH 03071
603-878-1713

Jeff's Collectibles
2318 S. 72nd St.
Lincoln, NE 68506
402-489-1800

Key-Aid Distributors
1739 W. Main St.
Ephrata, PA 17522
717-738-4241

Mike Silver
509 Danielle Ct.
Roseville, CA 95747
916-782-4800

Motorsport Direct
9260 Isaac St., Ste C
Santee, CA 92071
619-449-6712

Peter St.Yves
10 Fieldstone Dr.
Lakeville, MA 02347
508-947-3911

Phoenix Model Co.
P.O. Box 15390
Brooksville, FL 34609
352-754-8522

RCM Collectibles
2045 Cromwell Dr.
Wheaton, IL 60187
800-969-0723

Toys Plus
2353 N. Wilson Way
Stockton, CA 95205
209-944-5790

Ty's Toys
8535 Hazel Ln.
Waterford, WI 53185
262-662-0742

Vintage Toys
American Memorabilia Inc.
7500 W. Lake Mead Blvd.
Las Vegas, NV 89128
800-430-0667

Collectorholics
15006 Fuller Ave.
Grandview, MO 64030
816-322-0906

Dennis Shoup
1119 S. Curtis Ave., Apt A4
Kankakee, IL 60901
815-932-5262

Early Adventure,The
445 Gallitin Rd.
Belle Vernon, PA 15012
724-379-5833

Frederick Ross
2128 N. 38th St.
Milwaukee, WI 53208
414-444-5836

Keystone Toy Trader
529 N. Water St.
Masontown, PA 15461
724-583-8234

Kirk White
P.O. Box 999
New Smyrna Beach, FL 32170
904-427-6660

Mark Clark
109 Newport Dr.
North Syracuse, NY 13212
315-458-8330

Michael Melito
29 Food Mart Rd.
Boston, MA 02118
781-662-2189

Serious Toyz
21 Sunset Trail
Croton On Hudson, NY 10520
914-271-4272

Stephen Sawchuk
2590 Allen Crescent
Brossard, PQ, Canada J4z 3
450-676-6424

Tom Lastrapes
6050 86th Ave.
Pinellas Park, FL 33782
727-545-2586

Tom Mayfield
390 Mount Lori Dr.
Highlands, NC 28741
828-526-1925

Yankee Peddler Antiques
5205 Grenock Dr.
Lothian, MD 20711
410-741-9080

Grand Pa's Attic
1409 Phillips Rd.
Matthews, NC 28105
704-845-1079

Wind-Up Toys
Steven Agin
P.O. Box 68
Delaware, NJ 07833
908-475-1796

Web Site Directory

The following are Web sites of interest to toy collectors.

Appraisers/Insurance
American Society of Appraisers
www.appraisers.org
Collectibles Insurance
www.collectinsure.com
eppraisals.com
www.eppraisals.com
International Society of Appraisers
www.isa-appraisers.org

Action Figures
21st Century Toys
www.21stcenturytoys.com
Action Figure Collectors
www.actionfigurecollectors.com
Action Figure Times
www.aftimes.com
Action Figure World
www.actionfigureworld.com
Action Figures Online
www.afotoys.com
Action Man
www.actionman.com
Amok Time
www.amoktime.com
Andgor Toy Company
www.andgor.com
Anime Zone
www.animezone.com
Bandai America
www.bandai.com
Beast Wars
www.beastwars.com
Diamond Comic Distributors
www.diamondcomics.com
Dr. Mego's Reproduction Page
www.drmego.com
Figures Toy Company
www.figurestoycompany.com

Flatt World Figures
www.flattworld.com
Full Moon Toys
www.fullmoontoys.com
Graphitti Designs
www.graphittidesigns.com
He-Man
www.he-man.org
Hero Central
www.herocentral.com
JAKKS Pacific
www.jakkspacific.com
McFarlane Toys
www.mcfarlane.com
John Marshall
www.toyzilla.com
Moore Action Collectibles
www.mooreaction.com
Original 1970s Mego Parts
www.amazing3rdplanet.com
Outer Limits
www.outerlimitstoys.com
Plastic Dreams
www.plasticdreams.com
Playmates Toys
www.playmatestoys.com
Resaurus
www.resaurus.com
Sideshow Toy
www.sideshowtoy.com
Toy Vault
www.toyvault.com

Auctions
Amazon.com
www.amazon.com
Andale
www.andale.com
Auction Bytes
www.auctionbytes.com
AuctionImage.com
www.auctionimage.com

Toy Shop Annual 2001

Auction Watch
www.auctionwatch.com
AuctionWeekly.com
www.auctionweekly.com
BOTB Auctions
www.botb.com
Bill Bertoia Auctions
www.bertoiaauctions.com
Butterfield & Butterfield
www.butterfields.com
Buynsellit
www.buynsellit.com
Christie's
www.christies.com
Collector Auctions
www.collectorauctions.com
Collectingchannel.com
www.gomainline.com
Collectors Universe
www.collectorsuniverse.com
CollectingNation.com
www.collectingnation.com
eBay
www.ebay.com
eHobbies auctions
www.eHobbies.com
eWanted.com
www.ewanted.com
Hake's Americana & Collectibles
www.hakes.com
Randy Inman Auctions
www.inmanauctions.com
James D. Julia
www.juliaauctions.com
Lost Toy Auctions
www.losttoyauctions.com
Manion's International
Auction House
www.manions.com
McMasters
www.angelfire.com/oh/mcmaster sauctions
Skinner
www.skinnerinc.com
SoldUSA.com
www.soldusa.com
Sotheby's Amazon.com
www.sothebys.amazon.com
Theriault's
www.theriaults.com
TV Toyland/It's Only Rock N Roll
www.itsonlyrocknroll.com
Worth Guide
www.worthguide.com

Barbie
Barbie Bazaar
www.barbiebazaar.com
Marl & B
www.marlbe.com
Mattel
www.barbie.com
MTW New Barbie Center
www.newbarbie.com
Sandi Holder's Doll Attic
www.dollattic.com

Clubs
Collector Online's Club Directory
www.collectoronline.com/club directory.shtml
M&M Collectors Club
www.mnmclub.com
Mechanical Bank Collectors of America
www.mechanicalbanks.org

Die-Cast Vehicles
Action Performance
www.goracing.com
Adkins Collectibles
www.adkinsstore.com
CB's Die-Cast Car Museum
www.cbsmuseum.com
Code 3 Collectibles
www.code3.net
Collectible Toys
www.ttowndiecast.com
Exoto
www.exoto.com
Franklin Mint
www.franklinmint.com
Full Grid
www.fullgrid.com
Hall's Guide
www.hallsguide.com
Hot Wheels/Mattel
www.hotwheels.com
The Hot Wheels Source
www.digiweb.com/~hwsguys
J&M Toys
www.jandmtoys.com
J&R Enterprises
www.diecastcarmodels.com
JLP Merchandising
www.mascr.com
MTR Enterprises
www.diecastmuscle.com
Maisto International
www.maisto.com
Matchbox
www.matchbox.com
Micro Motors
www.micro-motors.com
Motorsport Direct
www.motorsport-direct.com

Neil's Wheels, Inc.
www.neilswheels.com
Peachstate Collectibles
www.peachgmp.com
Phoenix Model Co.
www.phoenix-model.com
Playing Mantis
www.playingmantis.com
Racing Champions Ertl
www.racingchamps.com
RPMs
www.geocities.com/MotorCity/9088
Thos. J. Locke & Son
www.thosjlocke.com
Thor Tek
www.thortek.com
Toy Nutz
www.toynutz.com
Toys Plus
www.toysplus.net

Dolls
Alexander Doll Company
www.alexanderdoll.com
Denise Van Patten Dolls
www.dollymaker.com
Doll & Hobby Shoppe
www.doll-hobby.com
Doll Magazine
www.dollmagazine.com
D's Dolls
www.dsdolls.com

Farm Toys
Red Wagon Antiques
www.redwagonantiques.com
Farm Toys
farm-toys.com

Fast Food Toys
Fast Food Toys Collectors Club
www.netcore.ca/~gkillops/toys.html
Heathside Collectibles
www.heathtoys.com/bobbys
McDonald's Collector's Club
www.mcdclub.com

Games
Association of Game & Puzzle Collectors
www.agpc.org
Buffalo Games
www.buffalogames.com
Cadaco
www.cadaco.com
Endless Games
www.endlessgames.com
ExtravaGAMEza
www.extravagameza.com

Sega of America
www.sega.com
Talicor, Inc.
www.talicor.com
USAOPOLY
www.usaopoly.com
Wizards of the Coast
www.wizards.com

General Toy Sites
Antique Toys
www.antiquetoys.com/collecting.html
Antiques Oronoco
www.antiques-oronoco.com
Basic Fun
www.basicfun.com
Clint Young Productions
www.cyproductions.com
Dave Cohen & Associates, Inc.
www.showcaseshowplace.com
Dr. Toy
www.drtoy.com
Collectible.com
www.collectible.com
Collector's Planet
www.collectorspla.net
EHobbies.com
www.ehobbies.com
Fox Soldiers
www.foxsoldiers.com
Gobler Toys
www.goblertoys.com
Gotta Have It
www.got2haveit.com
House of Toys
www.houseoftoys.com
In the '80s
www.inthe80s.com
Intergalactic Trading Co.
www.intergalactictrading.com
J.T. Puffins
www.puffins.com
Kinder Haus Toys
www.kinderhaus.com
LEGO
www.legomindstorms.com
Maloney's Online Antiques
& Collectibles Resource
www.maloneysonline.com
Marx Toys
www.marxtoys.com
Mechanical Bank Zone
www.pond.com/~paris/homezone.htm
Oak Leaf Comics & Sportscards
www.dustcatchers.com
Ohio Art
www.world-of-toys.com

Planet Toys
www.planet-toys.com
Santa Barbara Antique Toys
www.antiquetoys.com
Serious Collector
www.seriouscollector.com
Silverlit Toys
www.silverlit.com
Team Big Wheel
www.en.com/users/roach/teambig wheel.html
This Old Toy's Fisher-Price Toys
Welcome Page
www.thisoldtoy.com
Time Tunnel Toys
www.timetunneltoys.com
Time Warp Toys
www.timewarptoys.com
Toy Source Worldwide
www.toysource.com
Toy Tent
www.toytent.com
Trendmasters
www.trendmasters.com
Truckaholic
www.truckaholic.com
United Media
www.snoopy.com
U.S. Toy Company
www.ustoy.com
Weeks Juvenile Products
www.weekstoys.com
Wholesalecases.com
www.wholesalecases.com
World of TV Toys, Classic TV Collectibles
www.tvtoys.com

G.I. Joe

The Bivouac
www.thebivouac.com
Club Hair for G.I. Joe
www.clubhairforjoe.com
Elite Brigade
www.elitebrigade.com
Good Stuff to Go
www.goodstufftogo.net
The Joe Depot
www.ewtech.com/gijoe
Master Collector
www.mastercollector.com
The Medic
www.gijoemedic.com
The Old Joe Infirmary
www.oldjoeinfirmary.com
Small Blue Planet
www.smallblueplanet.com
YoJoe
www.yojoe.com

Grading and Authenticating

Action Figure Authority
www.toygrader.com
Diecast Grading Service
www.diecastgrading.com

Model Kits

Fatman Productions
www.fatmanprod.com
GEOmetric Design
www.geometricdesign.com
Menagerie Productions
www.menagerieproductions.com
Monsters in Motion
www.monstersinmotion.com
Phoenix Model Co.
www.phoenix-model.com
Revell
www.revell-monogram.com
Sassy's Satellite
www.sassysatellite.com

Museums

Delaware Toy and Miniature Museum
www.thomes.net/toys
Museum of Advertising Icons, Creatability
www.toymuseum.com
Museum of the City of New York Toy Collection
www.mcny.org/toy.htm
Toy and Minature Museum of Kansas City
www.umkc.edu/tmm

Plush

Gund
www.gund.com
Limited Treasures
www.limitedtreasures.com
Liquid Blue
www.liquidblue.com
Peaceable Planet
www.peaceableplanet.com
Planet Plush
www.planetplush.com
Steiff USA
www.steiff-club.com
Ty, Inc.
www.ty.com

Publishers

Amazing Figure Modeler
www.amazingmodeler.com
Chronicle Books
www.chroniclebooks.com
Krause Publications
www.krause.com
Mobilia.com
www.mobilia.com

Running Press
www.runningpress.com
Schiffer Publishing
www.schifferbooks.com
Toy Cars & Models
www.toycarsmag.com
Tomart
www.tomart.com
Toy Shop
www.toyshopmag.com

Repairs
Battery Operated Toy Repair
www.gocities.com/randyk10/toyrepair.html
Classic Tin Toy
www.classictintoy.com
Randy's Toy Shop
www.randystoyshop.com

Robots
American Memorabilia
www.ami21.com
Mark Bergin
www.bergintoys.com
B9 Online.com
ww.b9online.com
Comet Toys/Robert Johnson
www.comettoys.com
Richard Johnson
www.futureone.com/~toys/toy.htm
Rocket USA
www.rocketusa.com

Shopping
After Hours Toys
www.recorder.ca/afterhours
Annie M's Collectibles
www.anniems.com
ArtoyClassic
www.ArtoyClassic.com
Billy Galaxy
www.billygalaxy.com
Cloud City
www.cloudcity.net
eToys
www.etoys.com
FAO Schwarz
www.faoswchwarz.com
Frantic City Toys
www.franticcitytoys.com
Fun Antiques
www.fun-antiques.com
Fun House Toys
www.funhousetoys.com

Ghoulie Motors
www.ghouliemotors.com
Hasbro
www.hasbrocollectors.com
House of Monsters
www.thehouseofmonsters.com
John's Collectible Toys & Gifts
www.johns-toys.com
K-B Toys
www.kbkids.com
Kaleden Online
www.kaleden.com
M&J Variety
www.mjvar.com
MJR Needful Thingz
www.mjrneedfulthingz.com
New Force Comics & Collectibles
www.newforcecomics.com
Old Stuff Mall
www.oldstuffmall.com
Old Tyme Toy Store & Star Wars Collectibles
www.toycollectibles.net
Plastic Dreams
www.plasticdreams.com
Replay Toys
www.replaytoys.com
Salmagundi Tin Toys
www.web-tek-net/tintoys
The Earth Collectible Toy Mall
www.theearth.net
The Final Frontier Toys
www.finalfrontiertoys.com
Toy Monster
www.toymonster.com
Toys Toys Toys
www.nyttt.com
Toys R Us
www.toysrus.com
Toy Treasures
www.toytreasures.com
Village Comics & Collectibles
www.villagecomics.com
Wah's Antiques
www.wahs.com.hk
Yankee Peddler
members.aol.com/yankeetoys/jdpage.html
Yesteryear Toys
www.yesteryeartoys.com

Shows
Antique World Shows
www.chicagotoyshow.com

Atlantique City
www.atlantiquecity.com
Chiller Theatre Show
www.chillertheatre.com
Collectors Fairs
www.collectorsfairs.com
FX
www.fxshow.com
High Speed Promotions
www.highspeedshows.com
International Collectible Exposition
www.collectibleshow.com
K&S Promotions
www.kspromotions.com
Sci-Fi Expo.com
www.scifiexpo.com
Sci-Fi Model Con
www.victorymodels.com
Toy Memories
www.toymemories.com
Wonderfest
www.wonderfest.com
Jess Zavala
www.zzonemall.com

Star Wars
Brian's Toys
www.brianstoys.com
Hidden Rebel Base
www.hiddenrebelbase.com
Lucasfilm
www.starwars.com
Sir Steve's
sirstevesguide.com
Star Wars Collector Union
www.collectorunion.com
Star Wars Auctions.Com
www.starwarsauctions.com

Vehicles
Alleyguide
www.alleyguide.com
Blue Diamond Classics
www.bluediamondclassics.com
Cowboys & Kidillacs
www.kidillacs.com
Dean's Model Kit and Toy Museum
www.toys-n-cars.com
Motor City Model Cars
www.motorcityusa.com
Pedal Toys
www.sominn.com
Slot Car Heaven
www.andysautosport.com

Manufacturers Directory

Have you ever wanted to reach a toy manufacturer but didn't know how? This list can help.

While not all-inclusive, this list includes many notable toy and toy-related companies currently in business. Remember, many companies will not comment on the secondary market values of their toys. Comments and questions should generally be directed to the customer service department.

21st Century Toys
Action figures, military figures
2037 Clement Ave. Bldg. 33
Alameda, CA 94501-1317
510-814-0719
www.21stcenturytoys.com

Acccoutrements
Toys and novelties
P.O. Box 30811
Seattle, WA 98103
425-349-3838
www.accoutrements.com

Action Performance
Die-cast cars
4707 E. Baseline Rd.
Phoenix, AZ 85040
602-337-3824
www.action-performance.com

Action Products International Inc.
Toys, robots
390 N. Orange Ave.
Suite 2185
Orlando, FL 32801
407-481-8007
www.apii.com

Aladdin Industries
Lunch kits
703 Murfreesboro Rd.
Nashville, TN 37210
800-456-1233

Alfa's Fuzzy Town
Plush toys
5971 Lakeshore Dr.
Cypress, CA 90630
800-542-9462

ALPI International
Squeezies, miscellaneous toys
1186 63rd St.
Oakland, CA 94608
510-655-6456

Applause
Plush, PVC figures
merged with Dakin in 1995
6101 Variel Ave.
Woodland Hills, CA 91365-4183
818-992-6000

Aristoplay
Toys and games
8122 Main St.
Dexter, MI 48130
800-634-7738
www.aristoplay.com

Austin Abbott Inc.
Storage boxes, miscellaneous
202 S. First Ave.
Highland Park, NJ 08904
732-247-4344
www.austinabbott.com

Bachmann Industries
Toy trains, planes
1400 E. Erie Ave.
Philadelphia, PA 19124
215-533-1600

Bandai America
Action figures
5551 Katella Ave.
Cypress, CA 90630
714-816-9500
www.bandai.com

Basic Fun
Key chains
1080 Industrial Hwy.
Southampton, PA 18966
800-662-3380
www.basicfun.com

Bburago
Die-cast vehicles
P.O. Box 221220
Hollywood, FL 33022
800-344-4406

Berk Co.
Foam toys, games, others
bought by JAKKS Pacific in 1999
2850 E. Cedar St., Suite B

Don't Miss!

Alexander Doll Company
www.alexanderdoll.com

Dolls
615 W. 131st St.
New York, NY 10027-7982
212-283-5900

> **Don't Miss!**
>
> **Binney & Smith**
> *www.crayola.com*
>
> Crayola products, Silly Putty
> P.O. Box 431, 1100 Church Lane
> Easton, PA 19042
> 610-253-6271

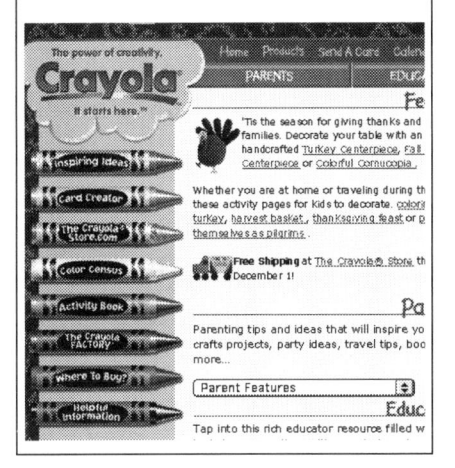

Ontario, CA 91761
909-923-0255

Brio Corp.
Developmental toys, others
N120 W18485 Freistadt Rd.
Germantown, WI 53022
414-250-3240

Buffalo Games
Games
220 James E. Casey Drive
Buffalo, NY 14206
716-827-8393

Bullyland
Prehistoric replicas, others
65W 55 Street 4 Floor
New York, NY 10019
212-974-9815

Cadaco
Games
founded 1935, previously known as Cadaco-Ellis
4300 W. 47th St.
Chicago, IL 60632-4477
312-927-1500
www.cadaco.com

Cardinal Industries
Games
21-01 51st Ave.
Long Island City, NY 11101
718-784-3000

Classic Metal Works
Die-cast vehicles
6465 Monroe St.
Suite 204
Sylvania, OH 43560
419-885-1448

Corgi Classics
430 West Erie
Suite 205
Chicago, IL 60610
800-800-CORGI

Craft House Corporation
Lindberg model kits
328 N. Westwood Ave.
Toledo, OH 43607-3343
419-536-8351

Danbury Mint
Die-cast vehicles
47 Richards Ave.
Norwalk, CT 06857-0001
203-853-2000

Darda, Inc.
Vehicle toys, etc.
1600 Union Ave.
Baltimore, MD 21211-1917
410-889-1023

Duncan Toys
Yo-yos
15981 Valplast Rd.
Middlefield, OH 44062
216-632-1631
www.yo-yo.com

Eastwood Automobilia
Distributor of die-cast vehicles, banks
Box 3014, Dept. PR
Malvern, PA 19355-0714
800-343-9353

Effanbee Doll Co.
Dolls
19 Lexington Ave.
East Brunswick, NY 08816
732-613-3852

Empire
Pre-school vehicles, others
acquired Buddy L in 1995
5150 Linton Blvd.
Delray Beach, FL 33484
561-498-4000

Endless Games
Games
22 Hudson Place, Room 1
Hoboken, NJ 07030
201-386-9465
www.endlessgames.com

Estes Industries
Models
1295 H St.
Penrose, CO 81240
719-372-6565

Exoto
Die-cast vehicles
5440 Atlantis Court
Moor Park, CA 93021
805-530-3830

Figures Toy Company
Action figures
15 Puritan Ave.
Cranston, RI 02920
401-946-5720
www.figurestoycompany.com

> **Don't Miss!**
>
> **Code 3 Collectibles**
> *www.code3.net*
>
> Die-cast vehicles
> 6115 Variel Ave.
> Woodland Hills, CA 91367
> 818-598-2298

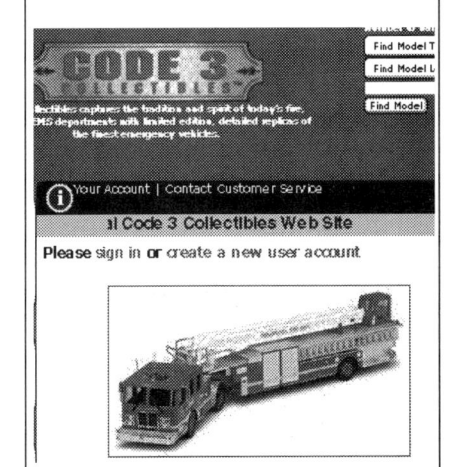

Toy Shop Annual 2001

> **Don't Miss!**
>
> **Galoob Toys**
> www.galoob.com
>
> Action figures, Micro-Machines
> *bought by Hasbro in 1998*
> 500 Forbes Blvd. S.
> San Francisco, CA 94080
> 415-873-0680

First Gear
Die-cast models
P.O. Box 52
Peosta, IA 52068-0052
319-582-2071

Fisher-Price
Plastic preschool toys, vintage wood pull toys
1930-present; division of Mattel
636 Girard Ave.
East Aurora, NY 14052
716-687-3449

Flatt World Figures
Action figures
P.O. Box 51790
Livonia, MI 48151
888-66-FLATT
www.flattworld.com

Flexible Flyer
Sleds
100 Tubb Ave., P.O. Box 1296
West Point, MS 39773
601-494-4732

Franklin Mint
Die-cast vehicles
Franklin Center, PA 19091-0001
800-523-7622

Full Moon Toys
Action figures
1645 N. Vine St., 9th Floor
Los Angeles, CA 90028
213-468-0599
www.fullmoontoys.com

Fun 4 All
Key chains, miscellaneous
156 Fifth Ave., Suite 823
New York, NY 10010
212-727-8833

G Whiz Enterprises
Lunch box repros
formerly Wonder Planet
14732 Lull St.
Van Nuys, CA 91405
626-683-9200

Gearbox Toys & Collectibles
Die-cast vehicles
4515 20th Ave. S.W.
Cedar Rapids, IA 52404
319-390-1405

GEOmetric Design
Vinyl, resin model kits
122 S. Wabasha St.
Suite 340
St. Paul, MN 55107
612-291-1909
www.geometricdesign.com

Gordy International
Miscellaneous
P.O. Box 2769
900 North Ave.
Plainfield, NJ 07062
908-755-9660

Graphitti Designs
Action figures
1140 N. Kraemer Blvd., Unit B
Anaheim, CA 92806-1919
800-699-0115
www.graphittidesigns.com

Gund
Plush
1898-present
1 Runyons Lane, P.O. Box H
Edison, NJ 08818
908-248-1500
www.gund.com

Hallmark
Kiddie Car Classics die-cast models
2525 Gillham Rd.
Kansas City, MO 64108-2622
816-274-8519

Hartland Plastics/Steven Manufacturing
Western/sports figures
224 E. Fourth St.
Hermann, MO 65041
314-486-5494

Hasbro Toy Group
Miscellaneous
1940s present; previously known as Hassenfeld Bros.; includes Kenner, Milton Bradley, Parker Brothers, Tonka, Playskool, Galoob
1027 Newport Ave.
Pawtucket, RI 02862-1059
401-727-5582
www.hasbrocollectors.com

Idea Factory
Plush
1350 Broadway, Ste. 2400
New York, NY 10018
212-564-7430

Irwin
Road race sets, games, others
2200 Corporate Blvd.
Suite 306
Boca Raton, FL 33431
561-988-0870
www.irwin-toy.com

JAKKS Pacific
Wrestling action figures, die-cast toys
22761 Pacific Coast Highway,
Suite 226
Malibu, CA 90265
310-456-7799
www.jakkspacific.com

Just Toys
Miscellaneous
20 Livingstone Ave.

JAKKS Pacific inc.

Dobbs Ferry, NY 10522
(914) 674-8697

Kenner Products
Action figures, G.I. Joe
Hasbro dropped name in 1999
615 Elsinore Pl.
Cincinnati, OH 45202
513-579-4927
www.hasbrocollectors.com

Kid Galaxy
Dolls, others
One Sundial Ave., Ste. 310
Manchester, NH 03103
603-645-6252
www.kidgalaxy.com

Krause Publications
Hobby magazines, books (*Toy Shop*, etc.)
1952-present
700 E. State St.
Iola, WI 54990
715-445-2214
www.krause.com

Larami Corp.
Miscellaneous
303 Fellowship Road, Suite 110
Mount Laurel, NJ 08054
609-439-1717

Legends In 3 Dimensions
2032 Armacost Ave.
Los Angeles, CA 90025
310-442-0156

LEGO Systems
Construction toys
555 Taylor Rd., P.O. Box 1600
Enfield, CT 06083-1600
203-763-6731
www.lego.com

Lionel Trains
Electric trains
1900-present
50625 Richard W. Blvd.
Chesterfield, MI 48051
810-949-4100
www.lionel.com

Little Tikes
Preschool toys
division of Rubbermaid
2180 Barlow Rd.
Hudson, OH 44236
216-650-3000
www.rubbermaid.com

Living Toys
Krofft, character toys
9107 Wilshire Blvd.
Suite 250
Beverly Hills, CA 90210
310-274-7669

Maisto International
Die-cast vehicles
7751 Cherry Ave.
Fontana, CA 92336
909-357-7988

Majorette Toys/Solido
Die-cast vehicles
2898NW 79th Ave.
Miami, FL 33122
305-593-6016

Marklin
Toy trains
distributor of German trains
16988 W. Victor Rd.,
New Berlin, WI 53151-0319
414-784-1095

Marx Toy Company
Miscellaneous
modern reincarnation of famed Louis Marx toy Company
249 E. Sebring Ave.
Sebring, OH 44672
330-938-8697

Matchbox Collectibles
Die-cast Vehicles
6000 Midlantic Dr.
Mount Laurel, NJ 08054
609-840-1511

Mattel Toys
Barbie, Hot Wheels
1945-present; acquired Tyco in 1997; acquired Pleasant Company in 1998

333 Continental Blvd.
El Segundo, CA 90245-5012
310-252-2000
www.mattel.com

McFarlane Toys
Spawn, other action figures
15155 Fogg St.
Plymouth, MI 48170
313-414-3500
www.spawn.com

MGA Entertainment
Games, interactive toys
16730 Schoenborn St.
North Hills, CA 91343
818-894-2525
www.mgae.com

Milton Bradley
Games
1860-present; division of Hasbro
443 Shaker Rd. E
Longmeadow, MA 01028-3149
413-525-6411

Minichamps USA
Die-cast vehicles
bought by Action Performance in 1998
14260 SW 136 St. Bldg. #7
Miami, FL 33186

Moore Action Collectibles
Action figures
3038 SE Loop 820
Fort Worth, TX 76140
817-568-2620
www.mooreaction.com

Nintendo of America
Video games
4820 150th Ave. NE
Redmond, WA 98052-5111
206-882-2040
www.nintendo.com

Norscot
Die-cast vehicles
10510 N. Port Washington
Mequon, WI 53092
262-241-3313

Nylint
Vehicle toys
1946-present
1800 Sixteenth Ave.
Rockford, IL 61104-5491
815-397-2880

OddzOn Products
Miscellaneous
purchased by Hasbro in 1997
50 Technology Court
Napa, CA 94558
707-251-3700

Ohio Art
Etch-a-Sketch, vintage tin toys
One Toy St.
Bryan, OH 43506
419-636-3141

Pac West
Mr. Octobears (plush)
7040 Avenida Encinas,
Suite 104-247
Carlsbad, CA 92009

Parker Brothers
Games

> **Don't Miss!**
>
> **Moore Action Collectibles**
> *www.mooreaction.com*
>
> Action figures, Micro-Machines
> *bought by Hasbro in 1998*
> 500 Forbes Blvd. S.
> San Francisco, CA 94080
> 415-873-0680

1880s-present; division of Hasbro
50 Dunham Rd.
Beverly, MA 01915
617-927-7600

Peaceable Planet
Plush
P.O. Box 23325
Savannah, GA 31403
912-651-8003
www.peaceableplanet.com

PEZ Candy
Candy dispensers
founded in 1927 in Austria
35 Prindle Hill Rd.
Orange, CT 06477
203-795-0531

Planet Plush
Plush
22 St. Joseph St.
Toronto, Canada M4Y 1J9
416-513-9464
www.planetplush.com

Playing Mantis
Johnny Lightning die-cast, model kits, action figures
3816 Grape Rd., P.O. Box 388
Mishawaka, IN 46545-2770
219-256-0300
www.playingmantis.com

Playmobil USA
Figures, play sets
22-E Nichols Ct.
Dayton, NJ 08810
908-274-0101
www.playmobil.com

Playskool
Preschool toys
division of Hasbro
1027 Newport Ave.
Pawtucket, RI 02862-1059

Poof Toy Products
Foam toys, Slinky
bought James Industries in 1998
45400 Helm St.
Plymouth, MI 48170
313-454-9552

Pressman Toy
Games
1920s-present
200 Fifth Ave., Suite 1052

> **Don't Miss!**
>
> **Playmates Toys**
> *www.playmatestoys.com*
>
> Action figures
> 611 Anton Blvd. #600
> Costa Mesa, CA 92626
> 714-428-2000

> **Don't Miss!**
>
> **Racing Champions/Ertl**
> *www.racingchamps.com*
>
> Die-cast vehicles, farm toys, banks
> 1945-present
> *purchased Ertl in 1999*
> Highways 136 & 20, P.O. Box 500
> Dyersville, IA 52040-0500
> 319-875-5607

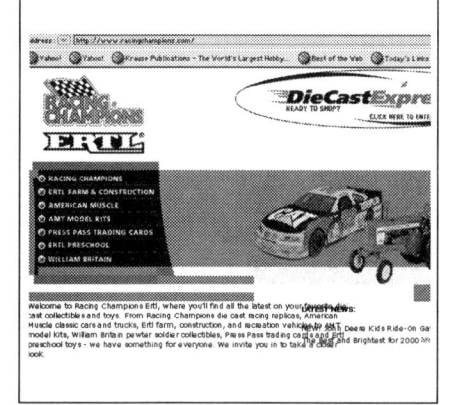

New York, NY 10010
212-675-7910

Radio Flyer
Wagons
6515 West Grand Ave.
Chicago, IL 60635
800-621-7613
www.radioflyer.com

Reeves International
Distributor of Breyer horses
14 Industrial Rd.
Pequannock, NJ 07440
201-694-5006

Rendition Figures
Action figures
16519 Wildnerness Rd.
Poway, CA 92064
619-592-6866

Resaurus
Action figures
240 Outerbelt St.
Columbus, OH 43213
614-751-9352
www.resaurus.com

Revell-Monogram
Model kits
8601 Waukegan Rd.
Morton Grove, IL 60053
708-966-3500
www.revell-monogram.com

Road Champs
Vehicle toys
division of JAKKS Pacific
7 Patton Dr.
West Caldwell, NJ 07006-6404
201-228-6900

Russ Berrie & Co.
Plush
111 Bauer Dr.
Oakland, NJ 07436
201-337-9000

Sanrio, Inc.
Hello Kitty, others
570 Eccles Ave.
So. San Francisco, CA 94080
650-925-2880

Schuco/Lilliput Motor Co.
Vehicles, tin
P.O. Box 447
Yerington, NV 89447
702-463-5181

Sega of America
Video games
255 Shoreline Dr.
Redwood City, CA 94065
415-508-2800
www.sega.com

Shadowbox Collectibles
Specialty figures
1578 N.W. 165th St.
Miami, FL 33169
305-621-0545
www.shadowboxinc.com

Sideshow Toy
Action figures, others
31364 Via Colinas, Suite 106
Westlake Village, CA 91362
818-879-1996

Smith-Miller
Vehicle toys
P.O. Box 139
Canoga Park, CA 91305
818-703-8588

SpecCast
Die-cast vehicles
428 6th Ave. NW
Dyersville, IA 52040-1129
319-875-8706

Steiff USA
Plush, teddy bears
founded in 1880 in Germany
P.O. Box 460
Raynham Center, MA 02768-0460
800-830-0429
www.steiffusa.com

Tamiya America
Miscellaneous
2 Orion
Aliso Viejo, CA 92656-4200
714-362-2240
www.tamiya.com

Thinkway Toys
Disney products, electronic banks, miscellaneous

> **Don't Miss!**
>
> **Revell-Monogram**
> *www.revell-monogram.com*
>
> Model kits
> 8601 Waukegan Rd.
> Morton Grove, IL 60053
> 708-966-3500

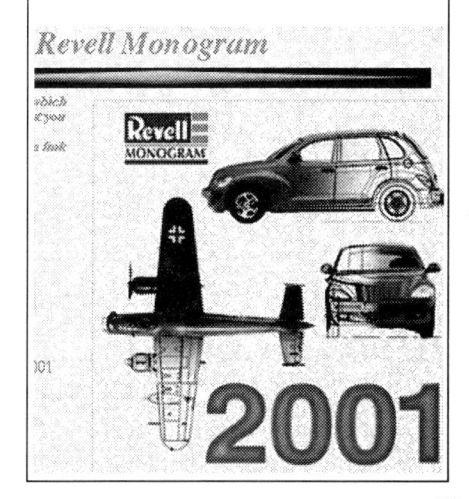

Don't Miss!

Ty, Inc.
www.ty.com

Beanie Babies
P.O. Box 5377
Oakbrook, IL 60522
800-876-8000

8885 Woodbine Ave.
Markham, Ontario Canada
L3R 5G9
905-470-8883
www.thinkwaytoys.com

Testors
Cars for sale, models
620 Buckbee St.
Rockford, IL 61104
815-397-2880

Tiger Electronics
Electronic games
purchased by Hasbro in 1998
980 Woodlands Parkway
Vernon Hills, IL 60061
847-913-8100

Today's Kids
Miscellaneous
formerly Wolverine
13630 Neutron Road
Dallas, TX 75244
972-404-9335

Tonka
See Hasbro

Tootsietoy / Strombecker
Vehicle toys, other
600 N. Pulaski Rd.
Chicago, IL 60624
312-638-1000

Toy Biz
Action figures
P.O. Box 90113
Allentown, PA 18109
800-634-7539

Toy Island
Miscellaneous
100 Universal Plaza Bldg. 10
Universal City, CA 91608
818-733-7500

Toy Vault
Action figures
P.O. Box 1915
London, KY 40743
606-864-8658
www.toyvault.com

Trendmasters
Action figures
611 North 10th St., Suite 555
St. Louis, MO 63101
314-231-2250

Tyco Industries
See Mattel

Uncle Milton Industries
Science, nature, exploration toys
5717 Corsa Ave.
Westlake Village, CA 91362
818-707-0800
www.unclemilton.com

U.S. Games Systems
Games, playing cards
179 Ludlow St.
Stamford, CT 06902
203-353-8400

USAOPOLY
565 Westlake St.
creator and distributor of specialty Monopoly games
Encintias, CA 92024
888-876-7659
www.usaopoly.com

Vital Toys
Action figures, other
PMB 386
269 S. Beverly Dr.
Beverly Hills, CA 90212
310-273-3782

Winross
Die-cast trucks
1965-present
Box 23860
Rochester, NY 14692
716-381-5638

Wizards of the Coast
Role-Playing Games, Pokémon, Magic: The Gathering
bought by Hasbro in 1999
P.O. Box 707
Renton, WA 98057
800-238-3114
www.wizards.com

X Toys
Action figures
27 Beach Road
Monmouth Beach, NJ 07750
732-870-1424

Zindart
U.S. distributor of Corgi
160 Sansome St., 18F
San Francisco, CA 94104
415-273-7094

2001 Toy Show Calendar

ALABAMA
Mar 10 2001 AL, Fairhope. March Fantasy Doll & Toy Show. Civic Ctr. Auditorium. SH: 9:30am-4pm, A: $2., $1. ages 6-12. Florence or Frances Brennan, PO Box 4123, Gulf Shores, AL 36547. PH: 334-968-7855.

ARKANSAS
May 5 2001 AR, Little Rock. 6th Annual All Doll & Toy Show. State Fairgrounds, Arts & Crafts Bldg., Roosevelt Rd., W. off I-30. SH: 10am-3pm, A: $3., under 12 free. Ruth Harvey, PH: 501-664-0470.

CALIFORNIA
Jan 6 2001 CA, San Jose. Super Toy Show. Napredak Hall, 770 Montague Expressway, near Hwy. 880. SH: 11am-4pm, A: $5. Time Tunnel Toys, PH: 408-298-1709.

Jan 13 2001 CA, Santa Rosa. Antique to Modern Dolls, Teddy Bears & Toy Show. Sonoma Cty. Fairgrounds, 1350 Bennett Valley Rd., Hwy. 101 to Hwy. 12 E., So. E St. exit. SH: 10am-4pm, A: $5., $2. 12 & under, 5 & under free. Golden Gate Shows, Fern Loiacono, PO Box 448, Mill Valley, CA 94942. PH: 415-383-2252 or FAX: 415-383-2292.

Feb 4 2001 CA, Petaluma. Pollyanna Doll Show. Veterans Memorial Bldg., 1094 Petaluma Blvd. S. SH: 10am-4pm, A: $4., under 12 free. Paula Huber, PH: 707-763-5237.

Feb 17 2001 CA, San Diego. 25th Annual Toys, Dolls, Bears, Clothes & Books Show. Scottish Rite Center, 1895 Camino del Rio S. SH: 10am-3pm, A: $5. Ruth Johnson, PH: 619-222-5335.

Feb 24 2001 CA, San Jose. Antique to Modern Dolls, Teddy Bears & Toy Show. Santa Clara Cty. Fairgrounds, 344 Tully Rd., Hwy. 101 to Tully Rd., Exit W. SH: 10am-4pm, A: $5., $2. 12 & under, 5 & under free. Golden Gate Shows, Fern Loiacono, PO Box 448, Mill Valley, CA 94942. PH: 415-383-2252 or FAX: 415-383-2292.

Mar 17 2001 CA, Marin County. Antique to Modern Dolls, Teddy Bears & Toys Show. Civic Ctr., Exhibit Hall, Ave. of the Flags, San Rafael, Hwy. 101 to N. San Pedro Rd. SH: 10am-4pm, A: $5., $2. 12 & under, 5 & under free. Golden Gate Shows, Fern Loiacono, PO Box 448, Mill Valley, CA 94942. PH: 415-383-2252 or FAX: 415-383-2292.

Apr 6-8 2001 CA, Nevada City. 18th Annual International Teddy Bear Convention. Miners Foundry, 325 Spring at Bridge St. A: $5., $3. seniors & students, under 12 free, SH: Fri. 12noon-5pm, Sat. 10:30am-5pm, Sun. 10:30am-2:30pm. Ted d'Bear, PO Box 328, Nevada City, CA 95959. PH: 530-265-5894 or FAX: 530-478-0728.

May 19 2001 CA, Santa Rosa. Antique to Modern Dolls, Teddy Bears & Toy Show. Sonoma Cty. Fairgrounds, 1350 Bennett Valley Rd., Hwy. 101 to Hwy. 12 E., So. E St. exit. SH: 10am-4pm, A: $5., $2. 12 & under, 5 & under free. Golden Gate Shows, Fern Loiacono, PO Box 448, Mill Valley, CA 94942. PH: 415-383-2252 or FAX: 415-383-2292.

Jun 2 2001 CA, San Jose. Antique to Modern Dolls, Teddy Bears & Toy Show. Santa Clara Cty. Fairgrounds, 344 Tully Rd., Hwy. 101 to Tully Rd., Exit W. SH: 10am-4pm, A: $5., $2. 12 & under, 5 & under free. Golden Gate Shows, Fern Loiacono, PO Box 448, Mill Valley, CA 94942. PH: 415-383-2252 or FAX: 415-383-2292.

COLORADO
Mar 11 2001 CO, Colorado Springs. Springs RMDTCA Toy Train Show. City Auditorium, Kiowa & Webber. SH: 10am-3pm, T: 150, A: $3., $5. family. Susan Deats, 1400 E. Orchard Rd., Littleton, CO 80121. PH: 303-798-2679.

Aug 11-12 2001 CO, Denver. Summer RMDTCA Toy Train Show. Holiday Inn, I-70 & Chambers Rd. SH: Sat. 11am-5pm, Sun. 10am-2pm, T: 200-250, A: $5., $8. family. Kim Vickery, 3040 S. Valentia St., Denver, CO 80231. PH: 303-337-9172.

Nov 24-25 2001 CO, Denver. Holiday Toy Train Show. Holiday Inn, I-70 & Chambers Rd. SH: Sat. 11am-5pm, Sun. 10am-2pm, T: 300, A: $5., $8. family. Bob Carlson, 3115 Isabell St., Golden, CO 80401. PH: 303-279-6258.

CONNECTICUT
Jan 7 2001 CT, Waterbury. Train Show. Sheraton, 3580 E. Main St., Rt. 84 E. Exit 25A, Rt. 84 W. Exit 26. SH: 9am-2pm, A: $4., 12 & under free with adult. Classic Shows, LLC, PO Box 2415, Shelton, CT 06484. PH: 203-926-1327.

Jan 21 2001 CT, New Haven. Annex Train & Scale Vehicle Show. Annex YMA Club, 554 Woodward Ave. SH: 9am-2pm, T: 85, A: $3., under 12 free. Frank Schiavonc, 20 Boston Ave., New Haven, CT 06512. PH: 203-467-3133.

Feb 4 2001 CT, Windsor Locks. Toy Soldier Muster Show.

Ramada Inn at Bradley Airport, 5 Ella Grasso Tpke. SH: 11am-4pm. D. Karppinen, PO Box 190-520, S. Richmond Hill, NY 11419. PH: 718-219-4919.

Feb 18 2001 CT, Wallingford. Train Show. Zandri's Stillwood Inn, 1074 S. Colony Rd., US Rt. 5, Exit 13 on I-91. SH: 9am-2pm, A: $4., 12 & under free with adult. Classic Shows, LLC, PO Box 2415, Shelton, CT 06484. PH: 203-926-1327.

Feb 18 2001 CT, Waterbury. A&M Collectible Toy Show. Sheraton, 3580 E. Main St., I-84E Exit 25A, I-84W Exit 26. SH: 9am-2pm, T: 100-8', A: $4., 8 & under free. Bernie, PH: 860-274-9592.

Mar 11 2001 CT, East Hartford. Diecast Model Vehicle & Antique Toy Show. Pratt Whitney Aircraft Club, 200 Clement Rd. SH: 9am-2pm, T: 120, A: $3. Bill McPherson, PH: 860-582-2939.

May 20 2001 CT, Windsor Locks. Toy Soldier Muster Show. Ramada Inn at Bradley Airport, 5 Ella Grasso Tpke. SH: 11am-4pm. D. Karppinen, PO Box 190-520, S. Richmond Hill, NY 11419. PH: 718-219-4919.

Sep 30 2001 CT, Windsor Locks. Toy Soldier Muster Show. Ramada Inn at Bradley Airport, 5 Ella Grasso Tpke. SH: 11am-4pm. D. Karppinen, PO Box 190-520, S. Richmond Hill, NY 11419. PH: 718-219-4919.

Dec 2 2001 CT, Windsor Locks. Toy Soldier Muster Show. Ramada Inn at Bradley Airport, 5 Ella Grasso Tpke. SH: 11am-4pm. D. Karppinen, PO Box 190-520, S. Richmond Hill, NY 11419. PH: 718-219-4919.

DELAWARE

Feb 4 2001 DE, New Castle. Automotive Toys & Models NASCAR Collectibles Show. Nur Temple, Rt. 13 N. at Rt. 40 Split. SH: 8:30am-2pm, T: 80, A: $3., under 12 free. High Speed Promotions, Steven Rosenzweig, 349 Windsor Dr., Cherry Hill, NJ 08002. PH: 856-667-6808.

FLORIDA

Jan 13-14 2001 FL, Palmetto. Doll, Bear & Beanie Show. Manatee Civic Ctr., US Hwy. 41. SH: Sat. 9am-4pm, Sun. 11am-4pm, A: $3.50, $2. children. PH: 941-722-6675 or 865-397-2544.

Jan 13 2001 FL, Tampa. Doll & Collectors Show. Holiday Inn Center City, 111 N. Fortune St. SH: 10am-4pm, T: 60, A: $5. PH: 407-402-1336 or 620-9231.

Jan 20 2001 FL, Pompano Beach. 26th Annual Doll, Bear & Toy Show. Civic Ctr., 1801 NE 6th St. SH: 10am-4pm, A: $3., under 12 free. Susan, PH: 305-652-8237 table info or Mildred, PH: 954-434-0818.

Jan 27 2001 FL, Deland. Central FL Farm Toy Show. Volusia Cty. Fairgrounds, I-4 btw. Orlando & Daytona, Exit 56 & Hwy. 44 E. SH: 9am-4pm, A: $2., under 12 free. John Rammacher, 1610 Park Ave., Orange City, FL 32763. PH: 904-775-2891 or Michael Booth, PH: 407-977-4488.

Jan 27 2001 FL, Melbourne. The Best Collectibles Show. Azan Shrine Temple, 1591 W. Eau Gallie Blvd. SH: 10am-4pm, T: 85, A: $2. Connie Holland, 324 NW Ontario St., Palm Bay, FL 32907. PH: 321-952-0835.

Feb 3-4 2001 FL, Orlando. 12th Annual FL Extravaganza Collectible Toy Show. Orange Cty. Conv. Ctr., 9800 International Dr. T: 1,200. Marz Productions, Inc., PH: 941-360-6666.

Feb 3 2001 FL, Ft. Meyers. The Magical Garden of Dolls Show. Araba Temple, 2010 Hanson St. SH: 10am-4pm, A: $3., 10 & under free. Beverly, PH: 941-542-7253 or Marte, PH: 941-549-2901 after July 15.

Feb 4 2001 FL, West Palm Beach. 7th Annual Toy Soldier & Action Figure Show. Airport Holiday Inn, 1301 Belvedere Rd. SH: 9am-3pm, T: 100, A: $5., $2. under 12. Frank Burns, PH: 561-732-7295 or FAX: 561-734-3842.

Feb 10-11 2001 FL, Lakeland. Central FL Auto Festival & Toy Expo. USA Int'l. Speedway, Rt. 33, Exit 20 off I-4. SP: 8:30am-4pm, T: 600, A: $4. Tom Conolly, 1056 Winifred Way, Lakeland, FL 33809. PH: 863-859-2180.

Feb 17 2001 FL, Tampa. Land 'O' Lakes Doll Show. Shrine Temple Unit Bldg., 4050 Dana Shores Dr. SH: 9am-4pm, T: 70, A: $2.50. Deborah Bigness, 6513 Westshore Cir., Tampa, FL 33616. PH: 813-839-7718.

Mar 17 2001 FL, Melbourne. The Best Collectibles Show. Azan Shrine Temple, 1591 W. Eau Gallie Blvd. SH: 10am-4pm, T: 85, A: $2. Connie Holland, 324 NW Ontario St., Palm Bay, FL 32907. PH: 321-952-0835.

May 12 2001 FL, Melbourne. The Best Collectibles Show. Azan Shrine Temple, 1591 W. Eau Gallie Blvd. SH: 10am-4pm, T: 85, A: $2. Connie Holland, 324 NW Ontario St., Palm Bay, FL 32907. PH: 321-952-0835.

Jul 14 2001 FL, Melbourne. The Best Collectibles Show. Azan Shrine Temple, 1591 W. Eau Gallie Blvd. SH: 10am-4pm, T: 85, A: $2. Connie Holland, 324 NW Ontario St., Palm Bay, FL 32907. PH: 321-952-0835.

Sep 29 2001 FL, Melbourne. The Best Collectibles Show. Azan Shrine Temple, 1591 W. Eau Gallie Blvd. SH: 10am-4pm, T: 85, A: $2. Connie Holland, 324 NW Ontario St., Palm Bay, FL 32907. PH: 321-952-0835.

Nov 17 2001 FL, Melbourne. The Best Collectibles Show. Azan Shrine Temple, 1591 W.

Eau Gallie Blvd. SH: 10am-4pm, T: 85, A: $2. Connie Holland, 324 NW Ontario St., Palm Bay, FL 32907. PH: 321-952-0835.

GEORGIA
Mar 25 2001 GA, Atlanta. Toy Show. Airport Marriott, 4711 Best Rd., College Park. SH: 10am-3pm, A: $5., $2. under 12. Marl, PH: 941-751-6275 or Joe, PH: 213-953-6490.

ILLINOIS
Jan 7 2001 IL, Grayslake. Skip's Car & Truck Cycle & Parts Swap Meet. Lake Cty. Fairgrounds, Rt. 45 & Rt. 120. SH: 8am-4pm. Skip's, PO Box 88266, Carol Stream, IL 60188. PH: 630-876-1042.

Jan 7 2001 IL, Bridgeview. If Its Got Wheels Swap Meet With Model Car Contest. John A. Oremus Community Ctr., 7900 S. Oketo Ave. SH: 9am-2pm, A: $3., under 10 free. Jim LaCoco, 231 Englewood Ave., Bellwood, IL 60104. PH: 708-544-1975.

Jan 7 2001 IL, Orland Park. Toys, Sports Card, Comic Book, Diecast & More Show. Civic Ctr., 1 blk. W. of LaGrange Rd. at 147th St. SH: 9am-2pm, T: 80-6', A: $1. John Leary, 9522 W. Shore Dr., Oak Lawn, IL 60453. PH: 708-423-1758.

Jan 14 2001 IL, Bridgeview. Toys, Comics, Hot Wheels, Beanies & Sports Card Show. Oremus Center, 2 blks. W. of Harlem Ave. at 79th St. SH: 9am-2pm, T: 65-8', A: $2. John Leary, 9522 W. Shore Dr., Oak Lawn, IL 60453. PH: 708-423-1758.

Jan 14 2001 IL, Rockford. Hot Wheels, NASCAR, Matchbox, Ertl & Diecast Show. Hoffman House at Holiday Inn, 7550 E. State St. (I-90, Exit Bus. 20). Russ Bambino, PH: 815-961-1223.

Jan 20 2001 IL, Orland Park. Toys, Sports Card, Comic Book, Diecast & More Show. Civic Ctr., 1 blk. W. of LaGrange Rd. at 147th St. SH: 9am-2pm, T: 80-6', A: $1. John Leary, 9522 W. Shore Dr., Oak Lawn, IL 60453. PH: 708-423-1758.

Jan 28 2001 IL, Naperville. Antique & Collectible Doll & Bear Show. Holiday Inn Select, 1801 Naperville Rd. (directly off I-88). A: $5., under 12 free. Gould & Gallup Promos., 525 W. Van Buren, Naperville, IL 60540. PH/FAX: 630-355-0574.

Jan 28 2001 IL, Orland Park. Toys, Sports Card, Comic Book, Diecast & More Show. Civic Ctr., 1 blk. W. of LaGrange Rd. at 147th St. SH: 9am-2pm, T: 80-6', A: $1. John Leary, 9522 W. Shore Dr., Oak Lawn, IL 60453. PH: 708-423-1758.

Feb 10 2001 IL, Orland Park. Toys, Sports Card, Comic Book, Diecast & More Show. Civic Ctr., 1 blk. W. of LaGrange Rd. at 147th St. SH: 9am-2pm, T: 80-6', A: $1. John Leary, 9522 W. Shore Dr., Oak Lawn, IL 60453. PH: 708-423-1758.

Feb 11 2001 IL, Rockford. Hot Wheels, NASCAR, Matchbox, Ertl & Diecast Show. Hoffman House at Holiday Inn, 7550 E. State St. (I-90, Exit Bus. 20). Russ Bambino, PH: 815-961-1223.

Feb 25 2001 IL, Orland Park. Toys, Sports Card, Comic Book, Diecast & More Show. Civic Ctr., 1 blk. W. of LaGrange Rd. at 147th St. SH: 9am-2pm, T: 80-6', A: $1. John Leary, 9522 W. Shore Dr., Oak Lawn, IL 60453. PH: 708-423-1758.

Feb 25 2001 IL, Wheaton. 37th Illinois Plastic Kit & Toy Show. Dupage Cty. Fairgrounds, Exhibition Ctr., 2015 W. Manchester Rd. SH: 9am-3pm, A: $4., $2. under 12. Past-Time Hobbies, Inc., PH: 630-969-1847.

Mar 10 2001 IL, Orland Park. Toys, Sports Card, Comic Book, Diecast & More Show. Civic Ctr., 1 blk. W. of LaGrange Rd. at 147th St. SH: 9am-2pm, T: 80-6', A: $1. John Leary, 9522 W. Shore Dr., Oak Lawn, IL 60453. PH: 708-423-1758.

Mar 11 2001 IL, Rockford. Hot Wheels, NASCAR, Matchbox, Ertl & Diecast Show. Hoffman House at Holiday Inn, 7550 E. State St. (I-90, Exit Bus. 20). Russ Bambino, PH: 815-961-1223.

Mar 25 2001 IL, Orland Park. Toys, Sports Card, Comic Book, Diecast & More Show. Civic Ctr., 1 blk. W. of LaGrange Rd. at 147th St. SH: 9am-2pm, T: 80-6', A: $1. John Leary, 9522 W. Shore Dr., Oak Lawn, IL 60453. PH: 708-423-1758.

Apr 1 2001 IL, Bridgeview. Toys, Comics, Hot Wheels, Beanies & Sports Card Show. Oremus Center, 2 blks. W. of Harlem Ave. at 79th St. SH: 9am-2pm, T: 65-8', A: $2. John Leary, 9522 W. Shore Dr., Oak Lawn, IL 60453. PH: 708-423-1758.

Apr 4 2001 IL, Rockford. Hot Wheels, NASCAR, Matchbox, Ertl & Diecast Show. Hoffman House at Holiday Inn, 7550 E. State St. (I-90, Exit Bus. 20). Russ Bambino, PH: 815-961-1223.

Apr 7 2001 IL, Orland Park. Toys, Sports Card, Comic Book, Diecast & More Show. Civic Ctr., 1 blk. W. of LaGrange Rd. at 147th St. SH: 9am-2pm, T: 80-6', A: $1. John Leary, 9522 W. Shore Dr., Oak Lawn, IL 60453. PH: 708-423-1758.

Apr 22 2001 IL, St. Charles. Antique-Collectible Toy & Doll World Show. Kane Cty. Fairgrounds, Rt. 64 & Randall Rd. SH: 8am-4pm, A: $6., under 12 free. Antique World Shows, Inc., PO Box 34509, Chicago, IL 60634. PH: 847-526-1645.

Apr 22 2001 IL, Orland Park. Toys, Sports Card, Comic Book, Diecast & More Show. Civic Ctr., 1 blk. W. of LaGrange Rd. at 147th St. SH: 9am-2pm, T: 80-6', A: $1. John Leary, 9522 W. Shore

Dr., Oak Lawn, IL 60453. PH: 708-423-1758.

May 6 2001 IL, Rockford. Hot Wheels, NASCAR, Matchbox, Ertl & Diecast Show. Hoffman House at Holiday Inn, 7550 E. State St. (I-90, Exit Bus. 20). Russ Bambino, PH: 815-961-1223.

May 12 2001 IL, Orland Park. Toys, Sports Card, Comic Book, Diecast & More Show. Civic Ctr., 1 blk. W. of LaGrange Rd. at 147th St. SH: 9am-2pm, T: 80-6', A: $1. John Leary, 9522 W. Shore Dr., Oak Lawn, IL 60453. PH: 708-423-1758.

May 27 2001 IL, Orland Park. Toys, Sports Card, Comic Book, Diecast & More Show. Civic Ctr., 1 blk. W. of LaGrange Rd. at 147th St. SH: 9am-2pm, T: 80-6', A: $1. John Leary, 9522 W. Shore Dr., Oak Lawn, IL 60453. PH: 708-423-1758.

Jun 3 2001 IL, Rockford. Hot Wheels, NASCAR, Matchbox, Ertl & Diecast Show. Hoffman House at Holiday Inn, 7550 E. State St. (I-90, Exit Bus. 20). Russ Bambino, PH: 815-961-1223.

Jun 9 2001 IL, Orland Park. Toys, Sports Card, Comic Book, Diecast & More Show. Civic Ctr., 1 blk. W. of LaGrange Rd. at 147th St. SH: 9am-2pm, T: 80-6', A: $1. John Leary, 9522 W. Shore Dr., Oak Lawn, IL 60453. PH: 708-423-1758.

Jun 24 2001 IL, St. Charles. Antique-Collectible Toy & Doll World Show. Kane Cty. Fairgrounds, Rt. 64 & Randall Rd. SH: 8am-4pm, A: $6., under 12 free. Antique World Shows, Inc., PO Box 34509, Chicago, IL 60634. PH: 847-526-1645.

Jun 24 2001 IL, Orland Park. Toys, Sports Card, Comic Book, Diecast & More Show. Civic Ctr., 1 blk. W. of LaGrange Rd. at 147th St. SH: 9am-2pm, T: 80-6', A: $1. John Leary, 9522 W. Shore Dr., Oak Lawn, IL 60453. PH: 708-423-1758.

Jul 8 2001 IL, Rockford. Hot Wheels, NASCAR, Matchbox, Ertl & Diecast Show. Hoffman House at Holiday Inn, 7550 E. State St. (I-90, Exit Bus. 20). Russ Bambino, PH: 815-961-1223.

Aug 5 2001 IL, Rockford. Hot Wheels, NASCAR, Matchbox, Ertl & Diecast Show. Hoffman House at Holiday Inn, 7550 E. State St. (I-90, Exit Bus. 20). Russ Bambino, PH: 815-961-1223.

Sep 16 2001 IL, Rockford. Hot Wheels, NASCAR, Matchbox, Ertl & Diecast Show. Hoffman House at Holiday Inn, 7550 E. State St. (I-90, Exit Bus. 20). Russ Bambino, PH: 815-961-1223.

Oct 7 2001 IL, Rockford. Hot Wheels, NASCAR, Matchbox, Ertl & Diecast Show. Hoffman House at Holiday Inn, 7550 E. State St. (I-90, Exit Bus. 20). Russ Bambino, PH: 815-961-1223.

Oct 28 2001 IL, St. Charles. Antique-Collectible Toy & Doll World Show. Kane Cty. Fairgrounds, Rt. 64 & Randall Rd. SH: 8am-4pm, A: $6., under 12 free. Antique World Shows, Inc., PO Box 34509, Chicago, IL 60634. PH: 847-526-1645.

Nov 4 2001 IL, Rockford. Hot Wheels, NASCAR, Matchbox, Ertl & Diecast Show. Hoffman House at Holiday Inn, 7550 E. State St. (I-90, Exit Bus. 20). Russ Bambino, PH: 815-961-1223.

Dec 2 2001 IL, Rockford. Hot Wheels, NASCAR, Matchbox, Ertl & Diecast Show. Hoffman House at Holiday Inn, 7550 E. State St. (I-90, Exit Bus. 20). Russ Bambino, PH: 815-961-1223.

INDIANA

Mar 12 2001 IN, Fort Wayne. Train & Collectable Toy Show. The Lantern, 4420 Ardmore. SH: 11am-4pm, T: 160, A: $2., under 12 free. Sally Valiton, 7112 Baer Rd., Fort Wayne, IN 46809. PH: 219-747-4485.

IOWA

Mar 11 2001 IA, Maquoketa. 19th Annual Doll, Toy & Bear Show. Jackson Cty. Fairgrounds, Jct. Hwys. 62 & 64. SH: 9am-4pm, A: $2.50, under 10 free. Dora Pitts, 4697 155th St., Clinton, IA 52732. PH: 319-242-0139.

Apr 7 2001 IA, Des Moines. 13th Annual Doll, Toy & Bear Show. Des Moines Christian School, 13007 Douglas Ave. SH: 9am-4pm, A: $3., under 10 free. Dora Pitts, 4697 155th St., Clinton, IA 52732. PH: 319-242-0139.

MARYLAND

Mar 3-4 2001 MD, Gaithersburg. Greater Washington DC Toys & Autograph Coll. Show. Holiday Inn. SH: 10am-5pm. JD Productions, PO Box 726, Cherry Hill, NJ 08003. PH: 856-795-0436 or FAX: 856-795-1475.

MASSACHUSETTS

Feb 11 2001 MA, Dedham. Antique & Collectible Toy Show. Holiday Inn, Rt. 1, Exit 15A. SH: 9am-2:30pm, A: $4.50. Mrs. Devlin, PH: 508-379-9733.

Mar 3-4 2001 MA, Boston. Monster Modelfest, Model & Garage Kit Expo. Holiday Inn, Rt. 1A, 225 Williams McClellan Hwy. SH: 10am-3pm, T: 60, A: $10., under 10 free with adult. Garagekit.com, 150 Vine St., Reading, MA 01867. PH: 781-944-5528.

Apr 8 2001 MA, Dedham. Annual Spring Antique & Collectible Toy Show. Holiday Inn, Rt. 1, Exit 15A. SH: 9am-2:30pm, A: $4.50. Mrs. Devlin, PH: 508-379-9733.

Apr 8 2001 MA, Peabody. 16th East MA Models & Toy Show. Holiday Inn, 1 Newbury St. (Rt. 1 N.). SH: 9am-2pm, T: 60, A: $3.50, under 12 free. Michael Zelikson, 24 Churchill Rd., Marblehead, MA 01945. PH: 781-631-9677 or 639-8466.

Apr 29 2001 MA, Boston.

Sunday Funnies Comic & Collectibles Show. Holiday Inn, Rt. 1A, 225 Williams McClellan Hwy. SH: 10am-3pm, T: 30-60, A: $5., under 10 free with adult. Garagekit.com, 150 Vine St., Reading, MA 01867. PH: 781-944-5528.

Jun 3 2001 MA, Boston. Sunday Funnies Comic & Collectibles Show. Holiday Inn, Rt. 1A, 225 Williams McClellan Hwy. SH: 10am-3pm, T: 30-60, A: $5., under 10 free with adult. Garagekit.com, 150 Vine St., Reading, MA 01867. PH: 781-944-5528.

Sep 29-30 2001 MA, Boston. Sunday Funnies Comic & Collectibles Show. Holiday Inn, Rt. 1A, 225 Williams McClellan Hwy. SH: 10am-3pm, T: 30-60, A: $5., under 10 free with adult. Garagekit.com, 150 Vine St., Reading, MA 01867. PH: 781-944-5528.

Oct 28 2001 MA, Peabody. 17th East MA Models & Toy Show. Holiday Inn, 1 Newbury St. (Rt. 1 N.). SH: 9am-2pm, T: 60, A: $3.50, under 12 free. Michael Zelikson, 24 Churchill Rd., Marblehead, MA 01945. PH: 781-631-9677 or 639-8466.

MICHIGAN

Jan 14 2001 MI, Novi. SMM Model Car & Toy Fair. Doubletree Hotel, I-96, Exit 162, 27000 Sheraton Dr. Bernie Wagers, PH: 248-684-5636 7pm-10pm.

Jan 21 2001 MI, Plymouth. Toy & Model Show. Cultural Center, 525 Farmer St. SH: 11am-3pm, A: $5., under 10 free. R.R. Promotions, Inc., PO Box 6094, Plymouth, MI 48170. PH/FAX: 734-455-2110.

Feb 11 2001 MI, Mt. Clemens. SMM Model Car & Toy Fair. Clintondale School, 35300 Little Mack. Bernie Wagers, PH: 248-684-5636 7pm-10pm.

Mar 10 2001 MI, Grand Rapids. Antique Toy & Toy Collectibles Show. Grand Valley Armory, 1200 44th St. SH: 9am-4pm, A: $2.50, 12 & under free with adult. G.R.A.T.C. Shows, 2437 Palmdale, Grandville, MI 49418. PH/FAX: 616-261-5664.

Mar 25 2001 MI, Livonia. Spring Toy Show. Monaghan K of C, 19801 Farmington Rd. SH: 10am-3pm, T: 65, A: $3. Stan Wutka, 5985 Leland Dr., Ann Arbor, MI 48105. PH: 734-747-7192.

Oct 21 2001 MI, Mt. Clemens. SMM Model Car & Toy Fair. Clintondale School, 35300 Little Mack. Bernie Wagers, PH: 248-684-5636 7pm-10pm.

Nov 10 2001 MI, Grand Rapids. Antique Toy & Toy Collectibles Show. Grand Valley Armory, 1200 44th St. SH: 9am-4pm, A: $2.50, 12 & under free with adult. G.R.A.T.C. Shows, 2437 Palmdale, Grandville, MI 49418. PH/FAX: 616-261-5664.

MINNESOTA

Jan 21 2001 MN, Brooklyn Center. 20th Annual Winter Doll, Bear & Miniature Show. Earle Brown Heritage Ctr., 6155 Earle Brown Dr. (I-694 & Hwy. 100). SH: 10am-4pm, A: $4., $1. under 12. Carol's Doll House, 10761 University Ave. NE, Blaine, MN 55434. PH: 763-755-7475.

NEVADA

Feb 25 2001 NV, Las Vegas. Joe & Marl Show. Gold Coast, 4000 W. Flamingo Rd. SH: 10am-3pm, A: $5., $2. under 12. Marl, PH: 941-751-6275 or Joe, PH: 213-953-6490.

NEW HAMPSHIRE

Jan 7 2001 NH, Nashua. Winter Doll Show. Elk's Lodge 720, 120 Daniel Webster Hwy., Exit 2 off Rt. 3. SH: 10am-3pm, A: $2.50, $1. children. PH: 978-342-8292.

NEW JERSEY

Jan 1 2001 NJ, East Brunswick. Toys, Sports Cards & Collectibles Show. Ramada Inn, Rt. 18 S. at the NJ Tpke., Exit 9. SH: 11am-5pm, T: 8', A: $2.50, $1.50 ages 6-12, under 6 free. Sallie Natowitz, PO Box 796, Matawan, NJ 07747. PH/FAX: 732-583-7915.

Jan 7 2001 NJ, Bellmawr. Automotive Toys & Models NASCAR Collectibles Show. Park Fire Company, 12 Essex Ave. SH: 8:30am-2pm, T: 65, A: $3., under 12 free. High Speed Promotions, Steven

Rosenzweig, 349 Windsor Dr., Cherry Hill, NJ 08002. PH: 856-667-6808.

Jan 14 2001 NJ, East Hanover. Greater NE Doll & Teddy Bear Winter Expo Show. Ramada Hotel, 130 Rt. 10 W. SH: 10am-4pm, T: 150. Yolanda Stanczyk, PO Box 368, Tannersville, PA 18372. PH: 570-620-2422.

Jan 21 2001 NJ, Piscataway. Doll & Bear Show. Sheraton Four Points, 21 Kingbridge Rd., I-287, Exit 9 to Centennial Ave. SH: 10am-4pm, A: $2.50, $1.50 ages 6-12. Sallie Natowitz, PO Box 796, Matawan, NJ 07747. PH/FAX: 732-583-7915.

Jan 28 2001 NJ, Wayne. The Great Bergen Passaic Toy & Train Show. P.A.L. Hall. SH: 9am-2pm, A: $5. Vic, PH: 631-653-8133.

Feb 11 2001 NJ, Freehold. Automotive Toys & Models NASCAR Collectibles Show. Nat'l. Guard Armory, 635 Rt. 33 (Business). SH: 8:30am-2pm, T: 78, A: $3., under 12 free. High Speed Promotions, Steven Rosenzweig, 349 Windsor Dr., Cherry Hill, NJ 08002. PH: 856-667-6808.

Feb 17-18 2001 NJ, Cherry Hill. TV, Film, Toys & Autograph Collectibles Show. Holiday Inn, Rt. 70 E. SH: 10am-5pm. JD Prods., PO Box 726, Cherry Hill, NJ 08003. PH: 856-795-0436 or FAX: 856-795-1475.

Feb 25 2001 NJ, Bordentown. Automotive Toys & Models NASCAR Collectibles Show. Nat'l. Guard Armory, Rt. 206 S. SH: 8:30am-2pm, T: 80, A: $3., under 12 free. High Speed Promotions, Steven Rosenzweig, 349 Windsor Dr., Cherry Hill, NJ 08002. PH: 856-667-6808.

NEW YORK

Jan 6 2001 NY, Sayville. Toys, Collectibles, Action Figures & Doll Show. Attias Indoor Flea Market, 5750 Sunrise Hwy. & Broadway. SH: 10am-6pm, T: 20, A: free. Paul DeCarlo, PH: 631-289-7398.

Jan 7 2001 NY, Hudson. Philmont Mountain Toy & Railroad Club Toy & Train Swap Meet. American Legion, 7 Fairview Ave. SH: 9am-2pm, A: $3. George Washburn, 40 Hudson St., Hudson, NY 12534. PH: 518-828-7902.

Jan 7 2001 NY, Brooklyn. Toy & Sports Card Show. Temple Hillel of Flatlands, 2164 Ralph Ave. SH: 10am-5pm, T: 50, A: free. Charles or Jeffrey Cerrito, PH: 718-368-4096 or 449-2375.

Jan 14 2001 NY, Elmont-LI. Model Train & Toy Show. St. Vincent De Paul School Auditorium, 1510 DePaul St. SH: 10am-3pm. Frank Deorio, 1500 DePaul St., Elmont, NY 11003. PH: 516-352-2127.

Jan 14 2001 NY, Queens. NY Toy Soldier Show. Radisson at JFK Airport, 135-30 140 St. D. Karppinen, PO Box 190-520, S. Richmond Hill, NY 11419. PH: 718-219-4919.

Jan 14 2001 NY, Brooklyn. Beanie Babies, Pokemon, Sports Card, Comics & Coll. Show. Golden Gate Inn, Knapp St. & Shore Pky. SH: 9am-3pm, T: 45-8', A: free. Mark Dillon, 222 Kings Highway, Brooklyn, NY 11209. PH: 718-266-1625.

Jan 20 2001 NY, Binghamton. Model Car Swap Meet. Comfort Inn, 1156 Upper Front St., Exit 6, Rt. 81. SH: 9am-3pm, A: free. Butch Somers, PH: 607-722-2716.

Jan 20 2001 NY, Sayville. Toys, Collectibles, Action Figures & Doll Show. Attias Indoor Flea Market, 5750 Sunrise Hwy. & Broadway. SH: 10am-6pm, T: 20, A: free. Paul DeCarlo, PH: 631-289-7398.

Jan 21 2001 NY, Brooklyn. Toy & Sports Card Show. Temple Hillel of Flatlands, 2164 Ralph Ave. SH: 10am-5pm, T: 50, A: free. Charles or Jeffrey Cerrito, PH: 718-368-4096 or 449-2375.

Jan 28 2001 NY, Freeport. Toy Memories Antique Toy Show. Recreation Ctr., 130 E. Merrick Rd. SH: 10am-3pm, T: 100, A: $5. Vinny Pugliese, PO Box 309, Albertson, NY 11507. PH: 516-593-8198.

Jan 28 2001 NY, Brooklyn. Beanie Babies, Pokemon, Sports Card, Comics & Coll. Show. Golden Gate Inn, Knapp St. & Shore Pky. SH: 9am-3pm, T: 45-8', A: free. Mark Dillon, 222 Kings Highway, Brooklyn, NY 11209. PH: 718-266-1625.

Feb 4 2001 NY, Syracuse. Collectorsfest-The Sports Memorabilia Show. State Fairgrounds, Horticutural Bldg., State Fair Blvd., Rt. 690, Exit 7. SH: 10am-4pm, T: 200-8', A: $3., under 10 free. Central NY Promos., 35 Hubbard St. Ste. 1, Cortland, NY 13045. PH: 607-753-8580 eves.

Feb 4 2001 NY, Brooklyn. Toy & Sports Card Show. Temple Hillel of Flatlands, 2164 Ralph Ave. SH: 10am-5pm, T: 50, A: free. Charles or Jeffrey Cerrito, PH: 718-368-4096 or 449-2375.

Feb 11 2001 NY, White Plains. The Great Westchester Toy & Train Show. Westchester County Center. SH: 9am-3pm, A: $7. George, PH: 518-392-2660.

Feb 11 2001 NY, Franklin Square-LI. Model Train & Toy Show. VFW Hall, 68 Lincoln Rd. SH: 9am-1pm. Rae Romano, PH: 516-486-6658.

Feb 11 2001 NY, Brooklyn. Beanie Babies, Pokemon, Sports Card, Comics & Coll. Show. Golden Gate Inn, Knapp St. & Shore Pky. SH: 9am-3pm, T: 45-8', A: free. Mark Dillon, 222 Kings Highway, Brooklyn, NY 11209. PH: 718-266-1625.

Feb 18 2001 NY, Brooklyn. Toy & Sports Card Show. Temple Hillel of Flatlands, 2164 Ralph Ave. SH: 10am-5pm, T: 50, A: free. Charles or Jeffrey Cerrito, PH: 718-368-4096 or 449-2375.

Feb 25 2001 NY, Brooklyn.

Beanie Babies, Pokemon, Sports Card, Comics & Coll. Show. Golden Gate Inn, Knapp St. & Shore Pky. SH: 9am-3pm, T: 45-8', A: free. Mark Dillon, 222 Kings Highway, Brooklyn, NY 11209. PH: 718-266-1625.

Mar 4 2001 NY, Brooklyn. Toy & Sports Card Show. Temple Hillel of Flatlands, 2164 Ralph Ave. SH: 10am-5pm, T: 50, A: free. Charles or Jeffrey Cerrito, PH: 718-368-4096 or 449-2375.

Mar 11 2001 NY, Franklin Square-LI. Model Train & Toy Show. VFW Hall, 68 Lincoln Rd. SH: 9am-1pm. Rae Romano, PH: 516-486-6658.

Mar 11 2001 NY, Brooklyn. Beanie Babies, Pokemon, Sports Card, Comics & Coll. Show. Golden Gate Inn, Knapp St. & Shore Pky. SH: 9am-3pm, T: 45-8', A: free. Mark Dillon, 222 Kings Highway, Brooklyn, NY 11209. PH: 718-266-1625.

Mar 18 2001 NY, Brooklyn. Toy & Sports Card Show. Temple Hillel of Flatlands, 2164 Ralph Ave. SH: 10am-5pm, T: 50, A: free. Charles or Jeffrey Cerrito, PH: 718-368-4096 or 449-2375.

Mar 18 2001 NY, Armonk. Westchester Toy Soldier Muster Show. Ramada Inn, 94 Business Park Dr., Corporate Park. SH: 10am-3pm. D. Karppinen, PO Box 190-520, S. Richmond Hill, NY 11419. PH: 718-219-4919.

Mar 25 2001 NY, Brooklyn. Beanie Babies, Pokemon, Sports Card, Comics & Coll. Show. Golden Gate Inn, Knapp St. & Shore Pky. SH: 9am-3pm, T: 45-8', A: free. Mark Dillon, 222 Kings Highway, Brooklyn, NY 11209. PH: 718-266-1625.

Apr 1 2001 NY, Elmont-LI. Model Train & Toy Show. St. Vincent De Paul School Auditorium, 1510 DePaul St. SH: 10am-3pm. Frank Deorio, 1500 DePaul St., Elmont, NY 11003. PH: 516-352-2127.

Apr 7 2001 NY, Syracuse. 25th Anniversary Doll & Teddy Bear Show. Knights of Columbus, 135 State Fair Blvd. SH: 10am-4pm, A: $3.50, $.75 children 12 & under. Peter Mylon, 601 Bradford Pky., Syracuse, NY 13224. PH: 315-446-6246.

Apr 8 2001 NY, Syracuse. Collectorsfest-The Sports Memorabilia Show. State Fairgrounds, Horticutural Bldg., State Fair Blvd., Rt. 690, Exit 7. SH: 10am-4pm, T: 200-8', A: $3., under 10 free. Central NY Promos., 35 Hubbard St. Ste. 1, Cortland, NY 13045. PH: 607-753-8580 eves.

Apr 8 2001 NY, Brooklyn. Beanie Babies, Pokemon, Sports Card, Comics & Coll. Show. Golden Gate Inn, Knapp St. & Shore Pky. SH: 9am-3pm, T: 45-8', A: free. Mark Dillon, 222 Kings Highway, Brooklyn, NY 11209. PH: 718-266-1625.

Apr 21 2001 NY, Binghamton. Model Car Swap Meet. Comfort Inn, 1156 Upper Front St., Exit 6, Rt. 81. SH: 9am-3pm, A: free. Butch Somers, PH: 607-722-2716.

Apr 21 2001 NY, New Hartford. Dolls of Disney. First United Methodist Church, 105 Genesee St. SH: 10am-4pm, T: 65, A: $3.50. Roma Welsh, 15 Beverly Pl., Utica, NY 13501. PH: 315-738-0922.

Apr 22 2001 NY, Brooklyn. Beanie Babies, Pokemon, Sports Card, Comics & Coll. Show. Golden Gate Inn, Knapp St. & Shore Pky. SH: 9am-3pm, T: 45-8', A: free. Mark Dillon, 222 Kings Highway, Brooklyn, NY 11209. PH: 718-266-1625.

Apr 28 2001 NY, New York. The Joe & Marl Show. Holiday Inn Rockville Centre, 173 Sunrise Hwy. SH: 10am-3pm, A: $5., $2. under 12. Marl, PH: 941-751-6275 or Joe, PH: 213-953-6490.

May 6 2001 NY, Syracuse. A Toyful Weekend-Antique & Collectible Toy Megashow. State Fairgrounds, Horticutural Bldg., State Fair Blvd., Rt. 690, Exit 7. SH: 9am-4pm, T: 500-8', A: $5., under 10 free. Central NY Promos., 35 Hubbard St. Ste. 1, Cortland, NY 13045. PH: 607-753-8580 eves.

May 6 2001 NY, Brooklyn. Beanie Babies, Pokemon, Sports Card, Comics & Coll. Show. Golden Gate Inn, Knapp St. & Shore Pky. SH: 9am-3pm, T: 45-8', A: free. Mark Dillon, 222 Kings Highway, Brooklyn, NY 11209. PH: 718-266-1625.

May 20 2001 NY, Brooklyn. Beanie Babies, Pokemon, Sports Card, Comics & Coll. Show. Golden Gate Inn, Knapp St. & Shore Pky. SH: 9am-3pm, T: 45-8', A: free. Mark Dillon, 222 Kings Highway, Brooklyn, NY 11209. PH: 718-266-1625.

May 27 2001 NY, Franklin Square-LI. Model Train & Toy Show. VFW Hall, 68 Lincoln Rd. SH: 9am-1pm. Rae Romano, PH: 516-486-6658.

Jun 3 2001 NY, Brooklyn. Beanie Babies, Pokemon, Sports Card, Comics & Coll. Show. Golden Gate Inn, Knapp St. & Shore Pky. SH: 9am-3pm, T: 45-8', A: free. Mark Dillon, 222 Kings Highway, Brooklyn, NY 11209. PH: 718-266-1625.

Jun 17 2001 NY, Brooklyn. Beanie Babies, Pokemon, Sports Card, Comics & Coll. Show. Golden Gate Inn, Knapp St. & Shore Pky. SH: 9am-3pm, T: 45-8', A: free. Mark Dillon, 222 Kings Highway, Brooklyn, NY 11209. PH: 718-266-1625.

Jul 1 2001 NY, Franklin Square-LI. Model Train & Toy Show. VFW Hall, 68 Lincoln Rd. SH: 9am-1pm. Rae Romano, PH: 516-486-6658.

Jul 1 2001 NY, Brooklyn. Beanie Babies, Pokemon, Sports Card, Comics & Coll. Show. Golden Gate Inn, Knapp St. & Shore Pky. SH: 9am-3pm, T: 45-8', A: free. Mark Dillon,

222 Kings Highway, Brooklyn, NY 11209. PH: 718-266-1625.

Jul 15 2001 NY, Brooklyn. Beanie Babies, Pokemon, Sports Card, Comics & Coll. Show. Golden Gate Inn, Knapp St. & Shore Pky. SH: 9am-3pm, T: 45-8', A: free. Mark Dillon, 222 Kings Highway, Brooklyn, NY 11209. PH: 718-266-1625.

Jul 21 2001 NY, Binghamton. Model Car Swap Meet. Comfort Inn, 1156 Upper Front St., Exit 6, Rt. 81. SH: 9am-3pm, A: free. Butch Somers, PH: 607-722-2716.

Jul 29 2001 NY, Brooklyn. Beanie Babies, Pokemon, Sports Card, Comics & Coll. Show. Golden Gate Inn, Knapp St. & Shore Pky. SH: 9am-3pm, T: 45-8', A: free. Mark Dillon, 222 Kings Highway, Brooklyn, NY 11209. PH: 718-266-1625.

Aug 5 2001 NY, Elmont-LI. Model Train & Toy Show. St. Vincent De Paul School Auditorium, 1510 DePaul St. SH: 10am-3pm. Frank Deorio, 1500 DePaul St., Elmont, NY 11003. PH: 516-352-2127.

Aug 12 2001 NY, Franklin Square-LI. Model Train & Toy Show. VFW Hall, 68 Lincoln Rd. SH: 9am-1pm. Rae Romano, PH: 516-486-6658.

Aug 12 2001 NY, Brooklyn. Beanie Babies, Pokemon, Sports Card, Comics & Coll. Show. Golden Gate Inn, Knapp St. & Shore Pky. SH: 9am-3pm, T: 45-8', A: free. Mark Dillon, 222 Kings Highway, Brooklyn, NY 11209. PH: 718-266-1625.

Aug 26 2001 NY, Armonk. Westchester Toy Soldier Muster Show. Ramada Inn, 94 Business Park Dr., Corporate Park. SH: 10am-3pm. D. Karppinen, PO Box 190-520, S. Richmond Hill, NY 11419. PH: 718-219-4919.

Aug 26 2001 NY, Brooklyn. Beanie Babies, Pokemon, Sports Card, Comics & Coll. Show. Golden Gate Inn, Knapp St. & Shore Pky. SH: 9am-3pm, T: 45-8', A: free. Mark Dillon, 222 Kings Highway, Brooklyn, NY 11209. PH: 718-266-1625.

Sep 9 2001 NY, Brooklyn. Beanie Babies, Pokemon, Sports Card, Comics & Coll. Show. Golden Gate Inn, Knapp St. & Shore Pky. SH: 9am-3pm, T: 45-8', A: free. Mark Dillon, 222 Kings Highway, Brooklyn, NY 11209. PH: 718-266-1625.

Sep 16 2001 NY, Syracuse. A Toyful Weekend-Antique & Collectible Toy Megashow. State Fairgrounds, Horticutural Bldg., State Fair Blvd., Rt. 690, Exit 7. SH: 9am-4pm, T: 500-8', A: $5., under 10 free. Central NY Promos., 35 Hubbard St. Ste. 1, Cortland, NY 13045. PH: 607-753-8580 eves.

Sep 23 2001 NY, Franklin Square-LI. Model Train & Toy Show. VFW Hall, 68 Lincoln Rd. SH: 9am-1pm. Rae Romano, PH: 516-486-6658.

Sep 23 2001 NY, Brooklyn. Beanie Babies, Pokemon, Sports Card, Comics & Coll. Show. Golden Gate Inn, Knapp St. & Shore Pky. SH: 9am-3pm, T: 45-8', A: free. Mark Dillon, 222 Kings Highway, Brooklyn, NY 11209. PH: 718-266-1625.

Oct 7 2001 NY, Brooklyn. Beanie Babies, Pokemon, Sports Card, Comics & Coll. Show. Golden Gate Inn, Knapp St. & Shore Pky. SH: 9am-3pm, T: 45-8', A: free. Mark Dillon, 222 Kings Highway, Brooklyn, NY 11209. PH: 718-266-1625.

Oct 20 2001 NY, Binghamton. Model Car Swap Meet. Comfort Inn, 1156 Upper Front St., Exit 6, Rt. 81. SH: 9am-3pm, A: free. Butch Somers, PH: 607-722-2716.

Oct 21 2001 NY, Brooklyn. Beanie Babies, Pokemon, Sports Card, Comics & Coll. Show. Golden Gate Inn, Knapp St. & Shore Pky. SH: 9am-3pm, T: 45-8', A: free. Mark Dillon, 222 Kings Highway, Brooklyn, NY 11209. PH: 718-266-1625.

Oct 28 2001 NY, Syracuse. Collectorsfest-The Sports Memorabilia Show. State Fairgrounds, Horticutural Bldg., State Fair Blvd., Rt. 690, Exit 7. SH: 10am-4pm, T: 200-8', A: $3., under 10 free. Central NY Promos., 35 Hubbard St. Ste. 1, Cortland, NY 13045. PH: 607-753-8580 eves.

Oct 28 2001 NY, Elmont-LI. Model Train & Toy Show. St. Vincent De Paul School Auditorium, 1510 DePaul St. SH: 10am-3pm. Frank Deorio, 1500 DePaul St., Elmont, NY 11003. PH: 516-352-2127.

Nov 4 2001 NY, Brooklyn. Beanie Babies, Pokemon, Sports Card, Comics & Coll. Show. Golden Gate Inn, Knapp St. & Shore Pky. SH: 9am-3pm, T: 45-8', A: free. Mark Dillon, 222 Kings Highway, Brooklyn, NY 11209. PH: 718-266-1625.

Nov 18 2001 NY, Freeport. Toy Memories Holiday Antique Toy Show. Recreation Ctr., 130 E. Merrick Rd. SH: 10am-3pm, T: 100, A: $5. Guy Demarco, PO Box 224, West Hempstead, NY 11552. PH: 516-593-8198.

Nov 18 2001 NY, Armonk. Westchester Toy Soldier Muster Show. Ramada Inn, 94 Business Park Dr., Corporate Park. SH: 10am-3pm. D. Karppinen, PO Box 190-520, S.

31st ANNUAL
BUFFALO, NY TOY SHOW
(Collectables & Antiques)

Sunday October 28, 2001
10:00 A.M. to 3:00 P.M.

HEARTHSTONE MANOR
333 Dick Road • Depew, New York

For table info write:
TOY SHOW
25 Tiernon Park, Buffalo, NY 14223
or Call 716-837-4023

Richmond Hill, NY 11419. PH: 718-219-4919.

Nov 18 2001 NY, Brooklyn. Beanie Babies, Pokemon, Sports Card, Comics & Coll. Show. Golden Gate Inn, Knapp St. & Shore Pky. SH: 9am-3pm, T: 45-8', A: free. Mark Dillon, 222 Kings Highway, Brooklyn, NY 11209. PH: 718-266-1625.

Nov 25 2001 NY, Syracuse. A Toyful Weekend-Antique & Collectible Toy Megashow. State Fairgrounds, Horticutural Bldg., State Fair Blvd., Rt. 690, Exit 7. SH: 9am-4pm, T: 500-8', A: $5., under 10 free. Central NY Promos., 35 Hubbard St. Ste. 1, Cortland, NY 13045. PH: 607-753-8580 eves.

Dec 2 2001 NY, Elmont-LI. Model Train & Toy Show. St. Vincent De Paul School Auditorium, 1510 DePaul St. SH: 10am-3pm. Frank Deorio, 1500 DePaul St., Elmont, NY 11003. PH: 516-352-2127.

Dec 2 2001 NY, Brooklyn. Beanie Babies, Pokemon, Sports Card, Comics & Coll. Show. Golden Gate Inn, Knapp St. & Shore Pky. SH: 9am-3pm, T: 45-8', A: free. Mark Dillon, 222 Kings Highway, Brooklyn, NY 11209. PH: 718-266-1625.

Dec 16 2001 NY, Brooklyn. Beanie Babies, Pokemon, Sports Card, Comics & Coll. Show. Golden Gate Inn, Knapp St. & Shore Pky. SH: 9am-3pm, T: 45-8', A: free. Mark Dillon, 222 Kings Highway, Brooklyn, NY 11209. PH: 718-266-1625.

Dec 30 2001 NY, Franklin Square-LI. Model Train & Toy Show. VFW Hall, 68 Lincoln Rd. SH: 9am-1pm. Rae Romano, PH: 516-486-6658.

NORTH CAROLINA

Jan 6-7 2001 NC, Charlotte. 12th Toy Collectors & Sportscard Show. Charlotte Hornet's Training Ctr., I-77 SC Exit 88, beside Knight's Castle BB Stadium. SH: Sat. 9am-4pm, Sun. 10am-4pm, T: 320-8', A: $5., 15 & under free. Inside Pitch, PH: 919-553-4285.

Jan 13-14 2000 NC, Raleigh. 5th NASCAR & Sportscard Collectibles Show. State Fairgrounds, Gov. Kerr Scott Bldg., 1025 Blue Ridge Rd. SH: Sat. 10am-5pm, Sun. 10am-4pm, T: 225-8', A: $3., 8 & under free. Inside Pitch, PH: 919-553-4285.

Jan 20-21 2001 NC, Raleigh. 37th North State Toy Collectors Show. NC State Fairgrounds, 1025 Blueridge Rd. SH: Sat. 9am-5pm, Sun. 10am-4pm, T: 285, A: $4. Carolina Hobby Expo, PH: 704-786-8373.

Sep 22-23 2001 NC, Greensboro. Greater Greensboro Doll & Bear Show. Coliseum. SH: Sat. 10am-5pm, Sun. 10am-4pm, A: $4. S. Clark, PH: 804-589-5400.

OHIO

Jan 5-7 2001 OH, Zanesville. Beanies, Sportscards, NASCAR & Collectibles Show. Colony Square Mall, 3575 Maple Ave. SH: Fri. & Sat. 10am-9pm, Sun. 12noon-6pm, T: 55-8', A: free. Jim Michaels, PO Box 8137, Zanesville, OH 43702. PH: 740-455-3121.

Jan 21 2001 OH, Eastlake. Railroad Show. North H.S., 34041 Stevens Blvd. SH: 10am-2:30pm, A: $4. Bob Frieden, 9695 Chillicothe Rd., Kirtland, OH 44094. PH: 440-256-8141.

Jan 28 2001 OH, Mansfield. Toy & Collectible Show. Richland Co. Fairgrounds, Trimble Rd. Exit off US Rt. 30. SH: 10am-4pm, T: 140-160. Kevin Spore, PO Box 9014, Lexington, OH 44904. PH: 419-756-3904 or Tim Babcock, PH: 419-884-3253.

Feb 11 2001 OH, Parma. Railroad Show. Senior H.S., 6285 W. 54th St. SH: 10am-2:30pm, A: $4. Bob Frieden, 9695 Chillicothe Rd., Kirtland, OH 44094. PH: 440-256-8141.

Feb 16-18 2001 OH, Zanesville. Beanies, Sportscards, NASCAR & Collectibles Show. Colony Square Mall, 3575 Maple Ave. SH: Fri. & Sat. 10am-9pm, Sun. 12noon-6pm, T: 55-8', A: free. Jim Michaels, PO Box 8137, Zanesville, OH 43702. PH: 740-455-3121.

Feb 25 2001 OH, Kirtland. Cleveland Collectible Toy Show. Lakeland College, I-90 & State Route 306. SH: 9am-2pm, A: $4. Bob Frieden, 9695 Chillicothe Rd., Kirtland, OH 44094. PH: 440-256-8141.

Mar 25 2001 OH, Mentor. Railroad Show. H.S., 6477 Center St. (State Rt. 615). SH: 10am-2:30pm, A: $4. Bob Frieden, 9695 Chillicothe Rd., Kirtland, OH 44094. PH: 440-256-8141.

Mar 30-Apr 1 2001 OH, Zanesville. Beanies, Sportscards, NASCAR & Collectibles Show. Colony Square Mall, 3575 Maple Ave. SH: Fri. & Sat. 10am-9pm, Sun. 12noon-6pm, T: 55-8', A: free. Jim Michaels, PO Box 8137, Zanesville, OH 43702. PH: 740-455-3121.

Apr 22 2001 OH, Mansfield. Toy & Collectible Show. Richland

Phone First!

Before you head off to that show — no matter how far the distance — you may want to call the show promoter first to confirm dates, times, places, number of dealers, etc. Last-minute changes may not always make it into our show listings. So to avoid any disappointment, always call first.

Co. Fairgrounds, Trimble Rd. Exit off US Rt. 30. SH: 10am-4pm, T: 140-160. Kevin Spore, PO Box 9014, Lexington, OH 44904. PH: 419-756-3904 or Tim Babcock, PH: 419-884-3253.

Apr 29 2001 OH, Columbus. Doll Show. Aladdin Temple, 3850 Stelzer Rd. SH: 10am-4pm, A: $3. Henrietta Pfeifer, 700 Winchester Pike, Canal Winchester, OH 43110. PH: 614-837-5573.

Jun 29-Jul 1 2001 OH, Zanesville. Beanies, Sportscards, NASCAR & Collectibles Show. Colony Square Mall, 3575 Maple Ave. SH: Fri. & Sat. 10am-9pm, Sun. 12noon-6pm, T: 55-8', A: free. Jim Michaels, PO Box 8137, Zanesville, OH 43702. PH: 740-455-3121.

Aug 19 2001 OH, Mansfield. Toy & Collectible Show. Richland Co. Fairgrounds, Trimble Rd. Exit off US Rt. 30. SH: 10am-4pm, T: 140-160. Kevin Spore, PO Box 9014, Lexington, OH 44904. PH: 419-756-3904 or Tim Babcock, PH: 419-884-3253.

Aug 31-Sep 2 2001 OH, Zanesville. Beanies, Sportscards, NASCAR & Collectibles Show. Colony Square Mall, 3575 Maple Ave. SH: Fri. & Sat. 10am-9pm, Sun. 12noon-6pm, T: 55-8', A: free. Jim Michaels, PO Box 8137, Zanesville, OH 43702. PH: 740-455-3121.

Oct 12-14 2001 OH, Zanesville. Beanies, Sportscards, NASCAR & Collectibles Show. Colony Square Mall, 3575 Maple Ave. SH: Fri. & Sat. 10am-9pm, Sun. 12noon-6pm, T: 55-8', A: free. Jim Michaels, PO Box 8137, Zanesville, OH 43702. PH: 740-455-3121.

Nov 4 2001 OH, Mansfield. Toy & Collectible Show. Richland Co. Fairgrounds, Trimble Rd. Exit off US Rt. 30. SH: 10am-4pm, T: 140-160. Kevin Spore, PO Box 9014, Lexington, OH 44904. PH: 419-756-3904 or Tim Babcock, PH: 419-884-3253.

PENNSYLVANIA
Jan 7 2001 PA, New Hope. Toy & Train Show. Egal Fire Co., Rt. 202 & Sugan Rd. SH: 8am-12noon, A: $3., under 12 free. Fred Dauncey, 1443 Leonard St., S. Plainfield, NJ 07080. PH: 908-755-7989 or 0346.

Jan 7 2001 PA, Gilbertsville. Train-O-Rama & Toy Show. Fire House, Rt. 73 (E. of Rt. 100). SH: 9am-2pm. Mary Preudhomme, 233 Long Lane Rd., Boyertown, PA 19512. PH: 610-367-7857.

Jan 21 2001 PA, Trevose. Antique & Collectible Toy Show. Radisson Hotel. SH: 10am-3pm, A: $6., $2. under 12 & over 65. PH/FAX: 718-428-0829.

Jan 28 2001 PA, Shrewsbury. Super Sunday Collectors Toy Show. Fire Hall. SH: 9am-1:30pm, T: 6', A: $2., under 12 free. Joe Golabiewski, PH: 410-592-5854 or Carl Daehnke, PH: 717-764-5411.

Feb 4 2001 PA, New Hope. Toy & Train Show. Egal Fire Co., Rt. 202 & Sugan Rd. SH: 8am-12noon, A: $3., under 12 free. Fred Dauncey, 1443 Leonard St., S. Plainfield, NJ 07080. PH: 908-755-7989 or 0346.

Feb 18 2001 PA, Gilbertsville. Train-O-Rama & Toy Show. Fire House, Rt. 73 (E. of Rt. 100). SH: 9am-2pm. Mary Preudhomme, 233 Long Lane Rd., Boyertown, PA 19512. PH: 610-367-7857.

Feb 25 2001 PA, Scotland. Train, Toy & Doll Show. Community Center, 3832 Main St. SH: 9am-3pm, T: 90, A: $2., under 12 free. Bill Robinson, 5678 Philadelphia Ave., Chambersburg, PA 17201. PH: 717-264-3081.

Mar 4 2001 PA, New Hope. Toy & Train Show. Egal Fire Co., Rt. 202 & Sugan Rd. SH: 8am-12noon, A: $3., under 12 free. Fred Dauncey, 1443 Leonard St., S. Plainfield, NJ 07080. PH: 908-755-7989 or 0346.

Mar 4 2001 PA, Shrewsbury. 41st Collector's Die Cast Toy Show. Fire Hall. SH: 9am-1:30pm, T: 6', A: $2., under 12 free. Joe Golabiewski, PH: 410-592-5854 or Carl Daehnke, PH: 717-764-5411.

Apr 1 2001 PA, New Hope. Toy & Train Show. Egal Fire Co., Rt. 202 & Sugan Rd. SH: 8am-12noon, A: $3., under 12 free. Fred Dauncey, 1443 Leonard St., S. Plainfield, NJ 07080. PH: 908-755-7989 or

---

2001
★ TOYS ★ COMICS ★
★ ALL CHILDHOOD COLLECTIBLES ★
ANTIQUE TIN & CAST IRON - MARX - ACTION FIGURES - SCI-FI - STAR TREK - STAR WARS - GOLD & SILVER AGE COMICS - NEW COMICS - COMIC CHARACTERS - MODEL KITS - 50's TO 70's TOYS - NOSTALGIA - CHARACTER DOLLS - BARBIE - G.I. JOE - FARM TOYS - DIE CAST - H.O. CARS - DINKY - CORGI - HOT WHEELS - BANKS - ERTL, FIRST GEAR & OTHERS - FANTASY - MOVIE & TV - TRAINS - TRAIN ACCESSORIES - DOLLS & ACCESSORIES - SPORTS AND NON-SPORTS CARDS

PITTSBURGH, PA
Pittsburgh Expo Mart At Monroeville Mall
Business Rt. 22 Monroeville,
Exit 6, PA Turnpike

MAY 5th & 6th
DEC. 1st & 2nd
SAT & SUN 10 to 4 both days

450 6-FT TABLES @ $55 each

ADMISSION: - Adults - $5.00 Kids under 12 - $3.00

Send to: **V. Crispin**
524 Rear Weldon St., Latrobe, PA 15650
(724) 537-5574

0346.

May 6 2001 PA, New Hope. Toy & Train Show. Egal Fire Co., Rt. 202 & Sugan Rd. SH: 8am-12noon, A: $3., under 12 free. Fred Dauncey, 1443 Leonard St., S. Plainfield, NJ 07080. PH: 908-755-7989 or 0346.

Aug 19 2001 PA, Gilbertsville. Train-O-Rama & Toy Show. Fire House, Rt. 73 (E. of Rt. 100). SH: 9am-2pm. Mary Preudhomme, 233 Long Lane Rd., Boyertown, PA 19512. PH: 610-367-7857.

Sep 2 2001 PA, New Hope. Toy & Train Show. Egal Fire Co., Rt. 202 & Sugan Rd. SH: 8am-12noon, A: $3., under 12 free. Fred Dauncey, 1443 Leonard St., S. Plainfield, NJ 07080. PH: 908-755-7989 or 0346.

Oct 14 2001 PA, New Hope. Toy & Train Show. Egal Fire Co., Rt. 202 & Sugan Rd. SH: 8am-12noon, A: $3., under 12 free. Fred Dauncey, 1443 Leonard St., S. Plainfield, NJ 07080. PH: 908-755-7989 or 0346.

Nov 11 2001 PA, New Hope. Toy & Train Show. Egal Fire Co., Rt. 202 & Sugan Rd. SH: 8am-12noon, A: $3., under 12 free. Fred Dauncey, 1443 Leonard St., S. Plainfield, NJ 07080. PH: 908-755-7989 or 0346.

Dec 9 2001 PA, New Hope. Toy & Train Show. Egal Fire Co., Rt. 202 & Sugan Rd. SH: 8am-12noon, A: $3., under 12 free. Fred Dauncey, 1443 Leonard St., S. Plainfield, NJ 07080. PH: 908-755-7989 or 0346.

SOUTH CAROLINA

Jan 6-7 2001 SC, Charlotte-Ft. Mill. 13th Annual Toy Collectors & Sportscard Show. Charlotte Hornets Training Facility, I-77, Exit 88 Gold Hill Rd. SH: Sat. 9am-4pm, Sun. 10am-4pm, T: 320. Ray Mozingo, PH: 919-553-4285.

TENNESSEE

Jan 7 2001 TN, Nashville. Hot Wheels Collectors Show. Super 8 Motel, I-24 & Harding Pl. SH: 9am-4pm, T: 40, A: free. Bruce Amato, PO Box 2821, Hendersonville, TN 37077. PH: 615-824-1752.

Mar 4 2001 TN, Nashville. Hot Wheels Collectors Show. Super 8 Motel, I-24 & Harding Pl. SH: 9am-4pm, T: 40, A: free. Bruce Amato, PO Box 2821, Hendersonville, TN 37077. PH: 615-824-1752.

Mar 31 2001 TN, Memphis. Toy & Doll Show. Agricenter Int'l., 7777 Walnut Grove Rd. SH: 10am-4pm, A: $3., $1. under 12. Productions Unlimited, 7334 N. May Ave., Oklahoma City, OK 73116. PH: 405-810-1010 or FAX: 405-810-0015.

May 6 2001 TN, Nashville. Hot Wheels Collectors Show. Super 8 Motel, I-24 & Harding Pl. SH: 9am-4pm, T: 40, A: free. Bruce Amato, PO Box 2821, Hendersonville, TN 37077. PH: 615-824-1752.

Jul 8 2001 TN, Nashville. Hot Wheels Collectors Show. Super 8 Motel, I-24 & Harding Pl. SH: 9am-4pm, T: 40, A: free. Bruce Amato, PO Box 2821, Hendersonville, TN 37077. PH: 615-824-1752.

Sep 9 2001 TN, Nashville. Hot Wheels Collectors Show. Super 8 Motel, I-24 & Harding Pl. SH: 9am-4pm, T: 40, A: free. Bruce Amato, PO Box 2821, Hendersonville, TN 37077. PH: 615-824-1752.

Nov 4 2001 TN, Nashville. Hot Wheels Collectors Show. Super 8 Motel, I-24 & Harding Pl. SH: 9am-4pm, T: 40, A: free. Bruce Amato, PO Box 2821, Hendersonville, TN 37077. PH: 615-824-1752.

TEXAS

Jan 13 2001 TX, Waco. Toy & Doll Show. H.O.T. Fairgrounds, General Exhibit Bldg., 4601 Bosque Blvd. SH: 10am-4pm, A: $2.50, .50. under 12. Productions Unlimited, 7334 N. May Ave., Oklahoma City, OK 73116. PH: 405-810-1010 or FAX: 405-810-0015.

Jan 13 2001 TX, Corpus Christi. 20th Jean Huff Doll & Toy Show. Bayfront Plaza Convention Center, Shoreline Dr. SH: 9am-4pm. Jean Huff, Claud Huff, 24779 County Rd. 11C, Mathis, TX 78368. PH: 361-547-3757.

Jan 20 2001 TX, Houston. Joe & Marl Show. Houston Marriott North at Greenspoint, 255 N. Sam Houston Pky. E. SH: 10am-3pm, A: $5., $2. under 12. Marl, PH: 941-751-6275 or Joe, PH: 323-953-6490.

Jan 20 2001 TX, Mesquite. Toy & Doll Show. Convention Ctr., 1700 Rodeo Dr. SH: 10am-4pm, A: $3., $1. under 12. Productions Unlimited, 7334 N. May Ave., Oklahoma City, OK 73116. PH: 405-810-1010 or FAX: 405-810-0015.

Feb 10 2001 TX, New Braunfels. Hill Country Doll Show. Civic Ctr., 380 S. Sequin St. SH: 9am-4pm, A: $3., $1. children. Dorothy Sojourner, 625 Gruene River Dr., New Braunfels, TX 78132. PH: 830-625-3245 or 608-0308.

Feb 17 2001 TX, Grapevine. Toy & Doll Show. Formerly Martha Gragg's, 1209 S. Main St. SH: 10am-4pm, A: $3., $1. under 12. Productions Unlimited, 7334 N. May Ave., Oklahoma City, OK 73116. PH: 405-810-1010 or FAX: 405-810-0015.

Feb 24 2001 TX, Gainesville. 15th Annual North TX Farm Toy Show. Civic Ctr., 311 S. Weaver. SH: 9am-3pm, A: $2., under 12 free with adult. Ed Pick, 504 CR 300, Muenster, TX 76252. PH: 940-759-2876.

Mar 3-4 2001 TX, Austin. Collectors Exposition. Crockett Ctr., 6301 Hwy. 290 E. SH: Sat. 9am-6pm, Sun. 10am-4pm, A: $3., under 12 free. Sally Wallace, 6702 Lexington Rd., Austin, TX 78757. PH: 512-454-9882.

Mar 24 2001 TX, Arlington. TX Collectorfest. Community Ctr. at Vandergriff Park, 2800 Matlock Rd. SH: 10am-4pm, T: 130, A: $2., kids free. Robert or Cindy Maston, PO Box 152, Red Oak, TX 75154. PH: 972-617-5044.

VIRGINIA

Feb 3-4 2001 VA, Virginia Beach. Toys, Comics & Sports Card Show. Pembroke Mall, Independence & VA Beach Blvds. SH: 11am-9pm, T: 100, A: free. Jason Tillman, PO Box 5480, Newport News, VA 23605. PH: 757-877-6204.

Feb 17-18 2001 VA, Roanoke. Valley Doll Show. Civic Ctr. SH: Sat. 10am-5pm, Sun. 10am-4pm, A: $4. S. Clark, PH: 804-589-5400.

Apr 1 2001 VA, Dunn Loring. 62nd Capitol Miniature Auto Collectors Club Show. Volunteer Fire House Community Hall, 2148 Gallows Rd. SH: 9am-1pm, A: $3., under 12 free. James William Brostrom, 6632 Cardinal Ln., Annandale, VA 22003. PH: 703-941-0373 or 301-434-6209.

Apr 21-22 2001 VA, Richmond. Mid-Atlantic Doll Expo. Raceway Complex, formerly State Fairgrounds. SH: Sat. 10am-5pm, Sun. 10am-4pm, A: $5. S. Clark, PH: 804-589-5400.

May 5-6 2001 VA, Virginia Beach. Toys, Comics & Sports Card Show. Pembroke Mall, Independence & VA Beach Blvds. SH: 11am-9pm, T: 100, A: free. Jason Tillman, PO Box 5480, Newport News, VA 23605. PH: 757-877-6204.

Aug 4-5 2001 VA, Virginia Beach. Toys, Comics & Sports Card Show. Pembroke Mall, Independence & VA Beach Blvds. SH: 11am-9pm, T: 100, A: free. Jason Tillman, PO Box 5480, Newport News, VA 23605. PH: 757-877-6204.

Oct 6-7 2001 VA, Virginia Beach. Toys, Comics & Sports Card Show. Pembroke Mall, Independence & VA Beach Blvds. SH: 11am-9pm, T: 100, A: free. Jason Tillman, PO Box 5480, Newport News, VA 23605. PH: 757-877-6204.

Nov 10-11 2001 VA, Richmond. Mid-Atlantic Doll Expo. Raceway Complex, formerly State Fairgrounds. SH: Sat. 10am-5pm, Sun. 10am-4pm, A: $5. S. Clark, PH: 804-589-5400.

Dec 1-2 2001 VA, Virginia Beach. Toys, Comics & Sports Card Show. Pembroke Mall, Independence & VA Beach Blvds. SH: 11am-9pm, T: 100, A: free. Jason Tillman, PO Box 5480, Newport News, VA 23605. PH: 757-877-6204.

WISCONSIN

Jan 21 2001 WI, Milwaukee. Scale Auto, Hobby & Toy Show. Serb Hall, 5101 W. Oklahoma Ave. SH: 10am-3pm, T: 250-8', A: $5. Unique Events, Jim Welytok, PH: 262-246-7171.

Jan 28 2001 WI, Milwaukee. Orphans In The Attic Doll, Toy & Bear Show. Serb Hall, 5101 W. Oklahoma Ave. SH: 10am-3pm, T: 140, A: $3.50, $1.50 ages 6-12. Marge Hansen, N96W20235 County Line Rd., Meno. Falls, WI 53051. PH: 262-255-4465.

Apr 8 2001 WI, Milwaukee. Orphans In The Attic Doll, Toy & Bear Show. Serb Hall, 5101 W. Oklahoma Ave. SH: 10am-3pm, T: 140. Marge Hansen, N96W20235 County Line Rd., Meno. Falls, WI 53051. PH: 262-255-4465.

CANADA

Jan 28 2001 ON, Mississauga. Annual Toy & Collectibles Show. Canadian German Club Hansa, 6650 Hurontario St. (1/4 mi. N. Hwy. 401).SH: 9:30am-2:30pm, T: 50, A: $5. Claus Gunzel, 525 Highland Rd. W., Ste. 304, Kitchener, ON N2M 5P4. PH: 519-570-3120.

Apr 22 2001 ON, Mississauga. 18th Annual Toronto Toy Show. International Centre, 6900 Airport Rd. SH: 10am-4pm, T: 350. Doug Jarvis, PH: 905-945-2775.

May 6 2001 ON, Ottawa. 12th Annual Spring Fantasy. Nepean Sportsplex, 1701 Woodroffe Ave. SH: 10am-4pm, A: $4.50, $3. seniors, $2. children with adult. Sue Foster, 124 Rothesay Dr., Kanata, ON K2L 1P1. PH: 613-836-5655.

Like to Surf the Net? Visit 'Toy Shop' Online

We realize many of our readers have computers and enjoy using them in collecting.

That's why Krause Publications, the publisher of *Toy Shop* and dozens of other collecting magazines and books, has made it easier for readers and subscribers to reach us.

Our general home page — **www.krause.com** — provides information about all our publications, including information on how to reach us and how to write for us. You can also learn more about Krause books — from automobiles to crafts to toys — on this site.

Access *Toy Shop* online directly at **www.toyshopmag.com**.

Toy Shop

Save $5 **Save $5**

Order Today! 1 yr (26 Issues) only $28.98

The Complete Marketplace for buyers and sellers of toys, models, figures and dolls. Thousands of easy-to-read, categorized classified ads, display ads and a complete editorial package.

To place a credit card order or for a FREE all-product catalog call

800-258-0929

Offer ABAX18

Toy Shop

M-F, 7 am - 8 pm • Sat, 8 am - 2 pm, CST
Mail orders on a 3x5 card to: **Toy Shop, Offer ABAX18**
700 E. State St., Iola, WI 54990-0001

www.toyshopmag.com

Toy Shop Annual 2001

Things you can do online...

search our classifieds for that missing item
for a job in the hobby field

order our latest books on collecting toys
a new subscription

renew your subscription to Toy Shop

find an answer to a nagging hobby question
the collectibles you want in our online classified ads

read all about your favorite collectibles

auction that item you don't need or find that elusive item

classified ads can be placed in Toy Shop
ads are also listed online

Toy Shop Annual 2001